DAMIEN

Hero of Molokai

DAMIEN

Hero of Molokai

by
Omer Englebert

St. Paul Books & Media

Library of Congress Cataloging in Publication Data

Englebert, Omer, 1893-

[Père Damien. English]

Damien, hero of Molokai / Omer Englebert. —3rd ed.

p. cm.

ISBN 0-8198-1870-4 (pbk.)

1. Damien, Father, 1840-1889. 2. Catholic Church—Hawaii—Clergy—Biography. 3. Missionaries—Belgium—Biography. 4. Missionaries—Hawaii—Biography. 5. Missions to lepers—Hawaii. I. Title.

BX4705.D25E56 1994

266'.2'092—dc20 94-4408

[B] CIP

Cover: painting of Fr. Damien by Edward Clifford

Translated by Benjamin T. Crawford

Revised, 1994 by Anne Eileen Heffernan, FSP

Printed and published in the U.S.A. by St. Paul Books & Media, 50 St. Paul's Avenue, Boston, MA 02130

St. Paul Books & Media is the publishing house of the Daughters of St. Paul, an international congregation of women religious serving the Church with the communications media.

1 2 3 4 5 6 7 8 9 99 98 97 96 95 94

Contents

Part One – Missionary to Hawaii

1. Roots and Early Years 11
2. First Years as a Religious 19
3. Voyage to Polynesia 29
4. The Hawaiian Islands 41
5. The District of Puna 51
6. The District of Kohala 61

Part Two – Among the Lepers

7. Molokai 85
8. “This is for Life” 95
9. Father to the Lepers 107
10. A Model Parish 127
11. World Fame and Hawaiian Honors 147

Part Three – Damien the Leper

12. Stricken 161
13. Final Labors 173
14. Friends 181
15. Trials 205
16. The Testimony of R. L. S. 219
17. Servant of the Lord 237
18. Death and Renown 245
Epilogue: A Miraculous Cure 261

PART ONE

Missionary to Hawaii

Chapter 1

Roots and Early Years

If on a map of Belgium you draw a straight line starting at Roubaix, passing through Waterloo, and extending to Aix-la-Chapelle, you divide the nation into two equal parts. At the same time, you trace the linguistic boundary between Flanders and Wallonia. To the north extends the Flemish or Teutonic zone of Belgium; to the south, the region that is French in language and culture.

Though the Flemings occupy a very small territory, they are in the first rank of peoples who have brought honor to Christian civilization and to humanity. Neither stains nor notable blunders tarnish their history. Never did anyone succeed in enslaving them, or in depriving them of their language or their faith. Hard-working, intelligent and gifted with exceptional adaptability, they have excelled in commerce and industry as well as in science and the arts. Their ancient towns preserve jewels of architecture; their school of painting is unique; their writers, musicians and hagiographers are distinguished in number and achievement. Moreover, in proportion to their numbers the Flemish people have furnished a notable recruitment of missionaries to the Church.

The district around Ninde-lez-Tremeloo is north of Waterloo and south of Antwerp, slightly closer to the latter. This countryside, through which flows the river Dyle, is flat, sandy and far from fertile, with some fields of heather and stands of fir. In that region Joseph de Veuster, the future Father Damien, was born on January 3, 1840.

The nineteenth-century inhabitants of the area were rugged and hard working. Everyone was a practicing Catholic; customs were wholesome; families were large; and vocations to the religious life were numerous.

Francis de Veuster, born in Tremeloo in 1800 and Anne Catherine Wauters, born in 1803 at Haecht, a neighboring market-town, had eight children. Two died at an early age; two, Leonce and Gerard, married; two, August and Joseph, became priests; and two, Eugenie and Pauline, joined the Ursulines. Joseph was the second to last child.

His parents farmed a bit of land in the country and on the side did some grain trading, which every other day brought the father to the markets of Louvain, Malines, Antwerp and Brussels. They dwelt in a modest house of red brick, separated from stables and carriage-sheds by a yard where pigs grunted and chickens pecked. They were sturdy, resolute Flemings, neither poor nor rich, but fervent in their faith and exemplary in their habits.

Boyhood

When Joseph was seven, he started school at Werchter, over a mile from Ninde. In all sorts of weather, he trudged there on foot. On Palm Sunday, 1850, in the parish church of Tremeloo, he received his First Communion.

There is not much to glean from this part of his life. In the eyes of his teacher, the lad was "very intelligent"; in those of his pastor, he was quite devout; and, in general, he seemed to be attentive to his duties.

In 1853, Joseph de Veuster was in his thirteenth year. He knew everything that was to be learned in the school at Werchter; he also knew how to cultivate land; he closed his books and stayed at home. Little by little the family circle had been shrinking. Already Eugenie, the elder girl, a religious since 1842, had passed to her eternal reward. Soon Pauline, in her turn, would become an Ursuline. And now there was preparation for another departure: August was taking Latin lessons to prepare him for his admittance into a junior seminary.

Soon only three children remained at home: three healthy boys, of whom Joseph was the youngest and the most efficient in all kinds of country chores. For four years he dug, he sowed, he harvested, he tended the cattle, he drove the team, he planted and pruned trees, he helped neighbors and he gained skill in the many handicrafts that a farmer must master to be self-sufficient.

The young farmer also enjoyed some prestige in the village, since he had more than ordinary strength and "lifted bags weighing over two hundred pounds as though they were nothing." His habits continued to be clean and his piety deep-rooted.

The family did not have enough resources to enable all the de Veuster sons to earn a living at home. So it was decided that Joseph would take up grain marketing like his father before him at Tremeloo and his godfather Goovaerts at Antwerp. It was intended that he go through a period of apprenticeship with the latter. However, it seemed wise for him to first learn French, so his people packed him off to Wallonia.

Braine-le-Comte

After the Easter vacation of 1858, Joseph became a boarder at the school of Braine-le-Comte in Hainault. This institution was under the direction of M. Derue-L'Hoir, a very respectable man and a good Christian, who did not require an excessive tuition fee from the parents of his pupils. In 1858, one was very well cared for by M. Derue-L'Hoir for a franc a day.

In Joseph's first letter to his parents, he bears witness to this fact and then expresses his contentment with the diet:

"Everything here is decent and quite comfortable. Every day we have a holiday meal, and the beer they serve us is excellent."

His letter is written in such faulty French as to require frequent correction and even rephrasing in order to render it understandable.

In time Father Damien would become multilingual, but he was always quite inaccurate in writing. He made no attempt, nor did he have any success, at writing well. His glory would be of a different order.

With the adaptability that we shall always observe in him, this youth of eighteen quickly accustomed himself to the new country and to his new life.

Learning French was important to him. He wanted to succeed as quickly as possible. On July 17, 1858, he deplored the distribution of prizes as an interruption to his studies: "I am sorry that it should arrive so soon with its aftermath; during the seven weeks of ensuing vacation, I shall forget the French I have learned."

Vocation

Why was he so bent on learning French? Would he need it in preparation for the priesthood? From this time on, if not from the time of his leaving Tremeloo, he had been hearing the call of God and was set upon following it. He had not as yet breathed a word of this. Premature confidences might put the whole matter in jeopardy. He who had trained himself to dispose of obstacles by sheer force, knew how to by-pass them as well.

There were many obstacles in the path of his vocation. The most serious of these were his backwardness in his studies and the anticipated opposition of his parents. It could be assumed that his father believed he had done his share for God by giving him three of his children. For Pauline had just followed August in embracing the religious life.

"What happiness she enjoys!" Joseph exclaimed in the letter of July 17; and he continued, indicating clearly enough the destination of his hopes: "I trust that my turn will come to choose the road I ought to take. Would it be impossible for me to follow my brother, Pamphile?"

Pamphile was the name in religion of August, who was now a brother in the monastery of the Sacred Hearts at Louvain.

Upon receiving this news item, the family concluded that something must have happened at Braine-le-Comte. As a matter of fact, a mission had just been preached there by some Redemptorist Fathers.

From his experiences at this mission, Joseph emerged inflexibly determined to become a religious. He thought first of entering La Trappe, and understandably the Trappist life could have appealed to him, with his personal blend of peasantry and austerity. He wrote of this to Brother Pamphile, who was then deep in the first fervor of his vocation.

One who has found the road to spiritual joy likes to lead others along it. Now, there is no one more happy than a young religious, nor, by the same token, is there anyone who throws himself or herself with more ardor into the making of proselytes. Without doubt, Pamphile replied that since the Congregation of the Sacred Hearts was near at hand, there was no need to look farther afield; one could sanctify oneself there quite as well as at La Trappe and, in addition, one could train to become a missionary. Undoubtedly Pamphile added that he would gladly help his brother gain admittance there.

Joseph decided to join his older brother as soon as possible. Did any resistance to his plan smolder in the family circle? A hint in that direction may be discerned in the following serious letter. It was written on Christmas, the day on which heaven seems to inspire everyone with good will. On this day it would be inappropriate to discourage Joseph in his desire to begin his novitiate without delay. Besides, the Redemptorist Father at the mission had repeated often enough that everlasting fire would punish parents who opposed the religious vocation of their children.

Braine-le-Comte

December 25, 1858

My dear Parents,

I must write to you on this beautiful day of Noel when I am convinced that God wishes me to leave the world to embrace the religious life. Adolescents, as well as children, owe obedience to their parents. Therefore, I come to ask your permission to follow my vocation, since I cannot set out upon that path without your consent.

Please don't think the idea of entering the holy religious state comes from me; I assure you that Providence has inspired me. You will not wish to place any obstacle in my way; if God calls me, I must obey; in refusing to answer the divine call, I should be exposing myself to eternal ruin; as for you, the Good God could punish you severely for your opposition to my following his will.

You know that the choice of a state in life determines our eternal happiness. My vocation, then, should not make you sad.

August (Pamphile) writes me that I shall surely be received at his monastery, but that I must not postpone discussing this matter with the superior beyond January 1, so that my novitiate may begin immediately afterwards.

Looking forward to that great happiness, I sign this as your obedient son,

J. de Veuster.

To induce them to agree, was it really necessary to threaten those good Christian parents with eternal damnation?

At any rate, the letter brought about the desired results. Joseph left Braine-le-Comte at once, and a few days later, in the company of his father, he went off to see his brother Pamphile at Louvain. So far as the parents were concerned it was only to be a visit of exploration. The two brothers, however, had lost no time. The accomplishment of the plans of their youngest son was farther advanced than the family at Tremeloo had imagined. For it was decided on the spot that Joseph would remain at the monastery and that his father was to return home alone.

Chapter 2

First Years as a Religious

On February 2, 1859, Joseph took the religious habit and changed his Christian name to Damien.

The Congregation which he had entered was, and is, officially called the Congregation of the Sacred Hearts of Jesus and Mary, but at that time people commonly designated it as the "Congregation of Picpus," since Picpus was the name of the street in Paris where Father Coudrin had established his first foundation in the days of Napoleon.

By the death of its founder, in 1837, the congregation had several hundred members. Today, these religious sons of Father Coudrin are spread across the globe. The priests devote themselves to teaching and preaching; the lay brothers apply themselves to manual work. All wear on the breast the image of the Sacred Hearts. Among other practices of devotion, these religious spend a half-hour before the Blessed Sacrament each day, and an hour a week in nocturnal adoration.

They established themselves at Louvain in 1840, the very year when, only ten miles away, the future Father Damien was born. In that college town they organized a novitiate and a house of studies for their recruits from Belgium, Holland and Germany.

Louvain

A heavy disappointment awaited Damien. He had arrived confident that he was on the road to the priesthood. However, it was pointed out to him that because he lacked a background in Latin, he was not prepared to master the studies required of the candidates for the priesthood. He was received, therefore, as a choir-brother. The choir-brothers, a subdivision no longer in existence, were given the care of chapels and similar duties on a level a little higher than that of the other lay brothers.

Disillusioned and humbled, our novice nevertheless refused to yield one iota of his plans. Since Pamphile was living under the same roof, Joseph had frequent opportunities to talk things over with him. Often they spoke of the difficulties a young man of nineteen can have in studying Latin. Here was a challenge which Damien accepted: to try to study and to retain in his memory some odd scraps of that difficult language. His attempt was quite successful. Thereupon, he begged his older brother to get permission to give him regular lessons. A former superior general of the Congregation had set down as one of the objectives "to give each member the opportunity of putting his talents to account." Since Damien had shown himself quite capable of making up for lost time in the study of Latin, Pamphile was allowed to do what his brother had so confidently asked.

The project was successful, for at the end of six months Brother Damien was translating *Cornelius Nepos* at sight. In the following year he was judged ready to pursue the course in philosophy, taught, as was customary, in the Latin tongue.

Despite this extraordinary effort, he did not neglect his

religious formation. Those who knew him in the novitiate have testified to his manly fervor in the service of God. "He was outstanding in his incomparable devotion to nocturnal adoration," recalls a fellow-student. "Thanks to his robust constitution, for a long time he began the nocturnal watch at three o'clock in the morning, or even at an earlier hour, without bothering to return to bed at its expiration. How often was I edified by his devout silence and his fervor! Like St. Paul, the first hermit, he was accustomed in his praying to utter gentle sighs that fell sweetly on the ear and quickened devotion in the souls of those nearby."

Light as they may have been, those sighs were not at all prescribed by the Rule nor encouraged by the master of novices. This master asked his disciple to have some regard for those around him, and to allow them in their prayers to savor without distraction the sweetness he savored in his.

In the museum at Tremeloo, one may see the lid of a writing desk into which three words have been carved with a jackknife: "Silence. Recollection. Prayer." They are the handiwork of Damien; the carving had been inspired by a spiritual conference on these three points. Again he was admonished, and was counseled to engrave on his heart, not on monastic furniture, the good resolutions made in the course of a sermon.

His taste for austerity urged him beyond the ordinary practices of the monastery. "One night when we were sleeping in the same room," relates Pamphile, "I awoke and saw a large bundle beside his bed. I went to see what it was. It was my brother, sleeping on the floor as the nearest thing, no doubt, to a board like the one he used at Tremeloo."

There are some men who cheerfully venture off the beaten paths, and there are others who, like workers on an assembly-line, incline rather to follow the customary way. The tendency of the first consists in drawing one's way of thinking, feeling and acting from within oneself rather than from others. It permits grappling with difficulties with a freshness of spirit and a fertility of imagination which often suffice to solve problems. Is it to his belated entrance into the monastery as well as to the comparatively brief time he spent there, that the hero of Molokai owed the preservation of his originality which, while it nourished in him a certain "divine discontent," also made his life so prodigiously successful in the long run?

Hilarem datorem diligit Deus. God loves to have people serve him with joy. Our novice was gifted with a cheerful temperament. His fellow-students used to call him "the good giant Damien," and his brother Pamphile tried to get him to "laugh a little less" — so exuberant was he in his joy — the joy of the pure of heart. We have Father Caprais' statement that in his role of novice master, he had "never encountered in [his] long experience a more sociable and lovable person."

The novice master adds that, from the first days of his religious life, the future leper had formed the plan of becoming a missionary in some distant land: "In the gallery of the chapel, there was a picture of St. Francis Xavier. One day I came upon him in prayer before this picture and asked him what he was doing there. 'I am asking the good God,' he said, 'through the intercession of St. Francis Xavier, to grant me the grace of being sent to the missions!' During his novitiate, he came every day, at the same hour, to kneel before this same picture."

Paris

At the end of June, 1860, Damien left Louvain for the novitiate at Issy in France, where it was customary for foreign candidates to spend the final days of their probationary period.

From Issy, he went to the Mother House in Paris, where on October 7, 1860, he pronounced his religious vows. Absorbing the traditions of his Congregation at that source, he studied philosophy there for a year, but did not neglect to improve his Latin and add a little Greek.

One of his fellow-students pictured him as "a man of bony frame, with broad shoulders and a large head, with a high forehead above full cheeks. His professor, also called him 'my big Damien.' His shortsighted peering eyes, however, soured just a little a countenance otherwise happy and agreeable."

Other eyewitnesses added that in the community he was like a fish in congenial water, passing from study to prayer to recreation with perfect ease, but allowing his predilection for work to carry him to extremes at times. He wished to make good the deficiencies occasioned by his late start, and his sound health permitted him, without perceptible harm, to prolong his nights of study.

Damien thought only of bringing his studies to a speedy conclusion in order to be able to "go among his savages." In the meantime, he lived happily with God in the observance of the Rule: every day, three hours of prayer, six to seven hours of study, three meals, two periods of recreation and once a week, a walk in the town or in the suburbs.

Matters outside his orbit held little interest for him. As would always be his habit, he plowed his own furrow, hoping that others would follow suit and feeling that it was not his job to take care of everything here below.

He wrote home: "Naturally, you would wish to be kept abreast of what is going on in Paris. But I do not read the newspapers; I am completely out of touch with politics and business. On Wednesdays, we go for a walk in the Bois de Vincennes.

"As for the walks in town, they no longer have for me the attraction they had at the beginning. I find them quite melancholy. Consequently, when there is any question about the section for our walk, I always leave the choice of streets to those who have more curiosity than I."

It is easy to understand how what he saw on the streets of Paris should shadow with worry and melancholy the mind of this unsullied youth.

So bitter is the spiritual combat that at times even a death that would appall a brave man takes on the color of a welcome deliverance. The theme of the "four last things" recurs time and again in the letters of Brother Damien.

On the occasion of a confrere's sudden death, he wrote: "I am aware that for a sinner the fear of what tomorrow may bring may be a mental torture, but for us exiles on earth yearning for the dissolution of the body, there is only joy in the thought that we are steadily advancing toward the hour when Jesus will say, 'Come, blessed of My Father!'"

However, our student, who was now at the advanced age of twenty, also had thoughts other than those of death. He was thinking especially of what he was going to do up to the time of death's summons. In his own mind, the matter was quite clear, but he was still concerned about preparing his parents to understand it. In one of his letters appeared some straws to show the wind's direction:

"The arrival of our missionary bishop has given us the opportunity of having a pontifical Mass on Easter Sunday.... The bishop will return soon to his mission in Oceania and will probably take one of us with him.... Would you not be happy if I were that one?"

This bishop was Tepano Jaussen, Vicar Apostolic of Tahiti. He had come back to France to publish a Tahitian dictionary, and he had stayed a considerable time at Picpus, where he had frequent talks with the students. One can imagine the absorption of Brother Damien as he listened to the tales of apostolic labors in the far-off South Pacific.

While waiting for the hour of release to go convert pagans, he tried his apprentice zeal on his father at Tremeloo, who in the worrisome task of gathering in his crops, did not give enough thought perhaps to the harvesting of merits for eternal life. Francis de Veuster was a worthy man and an edifying Christian. He even passed as a devout man, approaching as he did the communion rail four times a year, a noteworthy total in those days. But this did not deter our embryo missionary from stepping out of the seclusion of his cell to share the light he had received and to exercise the zeal he had not as yet put to practical use. A letter from that period shows this:

Paris, August, 1861

Dear Parents,

I have been happy to learn that all members of our family are in good health and that your business continues to prosper.

....Your soul as well as your body would profit if you were to neglect your material concerns a little so as to be able to devote more time to the business of your salvation. I am but carrying out a sacred duty in offering you this counsel.

As a more efficacious approach to your salvation, my very dear Father, you must receive the sacraments frequently, abstain from even small faults, be faithful in your morning and evening prayers and start no action without raising your heart to God, saying, 'Lord, it is for Your greater glory that I do this action.'

I urge you also to meditate every day on the love of God, on death, on the last judgment, on eternity, on the grievousness of sin, or on some other great truth. In this practice you would find help by reading a book of piety, such as *The Imitation of Jesus Christ* or *the Lives of the Saints*.

Forgive me, Father, for recommending things that you may judge difficult, perhaps, or impossible. But from the experience I have had with the mercy of God, I feel confident that with the grace of God you will be able to see the matter through. Besides, it is not you alone that I urge to follow this way of life. As a religious, I pass the advice on to all the members of my family. It will make me very happy to learn that you have not spurned my suggestions, but that you have turned them to good account....

Your very affectionate son,
Brother Damien.

This was quite a new way of life that Francis de Veuster found drawn up for him by his serious son. Probably he was satisfied that his son had found his own true vocation; but as for himself, the father would continue following his own vocation on a plane a little less sublime.

In due time, Francis and all his relatives, without their having asked for it, were enrolled in the Confraternity of the Blessed Scapular.

It happened on the day when Father Pamphile had sung his first Mass and was being honored by a family banquet. Toward the end of the meal, Brother Damien suddenly rose from his seat, drew from his pocket a bundle of scapulars and took advantage of the pious dispositions of the guests to urge them all to don these colors of the Blessed Virgin. "It is the finest souvenir," he said, "that you can take with you from this beautiful feast. Indeed, Father Superior is here with all the necessary faculties. Surely, you will not refuse such an opportunity." To be sure, no one declined.

After September 25, 1861, Damien was at Louvain again. The house where his last two years in Europe would slip away was directed by Father Wenceslas, a remarkable priest whose zeal for the promotion of studies at home did not diminish his interest in apostolic work abroad. He has testified that the future missioner applied himself diligently to the study of theology.

The students from Picpus attended the courses given at the university in the town. Because of the care with which he assimilated the subject matter, Damien seemed destined, in the eyes of some fellow-students, to become a professor. But Damien did not share this opinion. Far from studying for the sake of study itself, or for advancement in academic life, he held to his course of preparing himself for the missions.

Without casting any reflection on his memory, it can be admitted that Damien never contributed anything original to the clarification of Catholic doctrine. In the area of speculation, no one could be found more conformist than he. It was in the field of action that he displayed imagination and a taste for novelty.

Unlike many other self-taught persons who are inclined to boast, Damien was unusually humble. "When I look around at the lectures and see all these young men already far more learned than I," he said to his brother, "I feel that, without exaggeration, I do not belong here."

In the meantime, he kept up his practice of mortification. At noon, the students lunched at the second table, taking their places after their seniors had finished their meal. Occasionally by that time the meat had been consumed completely, or the portions that remained were small. Damien was never heard to complain about this. Rather, at times he was found slipping his portion to a neighbor with a huge appetite who was not hesitant in taking it—with thanks. Pamphile worried about his brother's health and scolded him for this practice. But the culprit kept repeating the offense, meeting all objections by taking double portions of soup and potatoes, of which there was no shortage.

It is not known how a certain bitter dispute arose one day among these young students. It was common knowledge, however, that Brother Damien did not find it easy to keep his indignation bottled up. "This is unworthy of the sons of the Sacred Hearts!" he shouted as he brusquely quit the group. The reproach had escaped before he thought of keeping it behind the wall of his teeth. His impetuous nature sometimes did him ill service, although he was careful to avoid injuring others. Furthermore, we have Father Wenceslas' word for it that he would lose no time in repairing the smallest harm. In regard to this failing, Father Jourdan observes that God often leaves in saints some imperfection or other to keep them humble and give them an opportunity for gaining greater merit.

Next to his monastery was a chapel dedicated to St. Anthony the Hermit. Through the course of centuries, it had suffered ill treatment. After the Revolution, it had served as a warehouse until 1847, when some Protestants bought it as a meeting-place. In 1862, the Picpus Fathers found themselves in a position to buy back the property and restore it to its original functions. On September 28, 1862, Bishop Tepano Jaussen rededicated this chapel. We may be sure that as Damien assisted at these rites he never imagined that in time to come, his own poor body, the willing victim of leprosy, would come to rest there and would be the object of the veneration of throngs of his fellow-men.

Chapter 3

Voyage to Polynesia

Bishop Maigret, Vicar Apostolic of the Hawaiian Islands, did not hide his concern over the scarcity of missionaries in his outpost.

In 1863, the superior general of the Congregation of the Sacred Hearts was induced to send reinforcements. Six men of Picpus and ten sisters would set out for Hawaii at the end of October. Father Pamphile was selected to go, for he too felt the call to be a missionary. In fact, it was in order to follow it that he had left the junior seminary at Louvain to enter the house of the Sacred Hearts.

Unfortunately, an epidemic of typhus broke out in Louvain. Forgetful of self, Pamphile went from bedside to stricken bedside, consoling the sick with the sacraments. Then, in his turn, he was laid low by the disease. He recovered so slowly that as the day of departure for the missions drew near, he seemed quite unfit to travel with the chosen band. Finally, all doubt was removed when the local superior, Father Wenceslas, took the advice of the attending physician and sent Pamphile back to the mother house under obedience. This was a heavy blow for the convalescent, who revealed the full weight of his disappointment to his brother, Damien.

Damien was struck with an idea. "Suppose I ask our superiors to let me go in your place?" The sick man nodded his approval. Damien lost no time in applying for the permission, writing directly to the superior general, so as to avoid the possible refusal of his immediate superior, Father Wenceslas.

There is no copy of his letter in existence, but the thrust of it is clear. Since Father Pamphile's ticket had already been paid for, holy poverty counseled that it be used. What could better solace the sore heart of Pamphile and perhaps hasten his recovery than knowing that his place would be taken by his brother? Finally, why doubt the will of God that showed itself in Brother Damien's glowing health and unshakable vocation?

We do not know the wording of his letter, but the father general was so impressed as to reply without delay. Only two days after Damien had sent the letter, Father Wenceslas approached the young brother as he sat at table and dropped before him the reply from Paris. "You are not backward about rushing ahead of your time to the missions, are you?" he remarked. It was true: the father general had granted the desired permission. Forgetting the restraints of religious modesty, Damien surprised his confreres by pushing aside his lunch and, mandate in hand, dashing upstairs to give the heartening news to the bedridden Pamphile.

The father general had advised Damien to hasten to Paris, where a retreat for the departing missionaries was about to begin. But first, without thinking even of finishing his interrupted lunch, the young man set out for Tremeloo.

Farewells and Departure

It was a hard and unexpected blow for his family to have to say good-bye for life. Never again here below would the aging parents see their youngest son, so affectionate and cheerful. He would sit no more at the family table; he would not be at hand to comfort their last hours and to close their eyes in death.

Joseph embraced his brothers and his sisters-in-law; for the last time, he clutched in his arms his father, bowed under the years. But he lacked the courage to make a clean and irrevocable break from his mother. "Mama, we shall meet again – soon," he said, forcing himself to appear light-hearted. "Tomorrow morning, I am going to Montaigu to say good-bye to Our Lady. Be there! I don't think you have gone there yet to thank the Blessed Virgin for having brought Pamphile back to health. I count on seeing you there. Come! Don't cry! Till tomorrow then, Mama!" And off he went quickly with a backward glance at the home he would never see again. Though he managed to keep a smile on his lips, he was choking back the sob in his throat.

He spent the last evening at Pamphile's bedside. Toward eleven p.m., he set out on the road to Montaigu.

One of the few elevations to rise above the Flemish plain, Montaigu is located near Diest. For centuries crowds have flocked there to implore the help of the Mother of God. In earlier days, the venerated statue was set in an oak, but since 1827 the ancient miraculous image had resided in a beautiful renaissance church. Gleaming in the light of countless candles, the statue had been surrounded by abandoned crutches and thousands of *ex voto* offerings set up by grateful pilgrims. In his boyhood days, St. John Berchmans had often knelt there in prayer.

The students of Picpus made yearly pilgrimages to this shrine. Since neither train nor tram came near this hallowed spot, the pilgrims had to set out at midnight to cover on foot the fifteen miles of road that would bring them to the sanctuary at dawn in time to receive Communion at the early Mass.

That night, Brother Damien made this journey for the last time – alone. In the half-light before dawn, he knelt at the feet of Our Lady, awaiting his earthly mother. That spry sexagenarian was not long in arriving, in the company of her daughter-in-law

Marie. As they had done many a time before, mother and son knelt side by side before the smiling face of Our Lady of Grace. Mother prayed for son; son for mother. She begged the Queen of Apostles to guard her dear boy whom the call of God was tearing from her loving arms. The tall son entrusted to her who is known to be the Consoler of the Afflicted his elderly mother, whose heart was bruised with grief.

Later on, the sister-in-law Marie related the rest of this episode.

"When we had finished our devotions, it was time to take to the road back to town. We left the church, his mother and I going ahead, while he walked a little to the rear, casting frequent glances back toward the sanctuary.

"'You are not in much of a hurry, son!' said his mother.

"'This is the last time I shall see this dear shrine. Let me feast my eyes a little longer. I have asked of Our Lady as a special favor the privilege of working on the mission a dozen years.'

"I noticed that he had his handkerchief in his hand to wipe away the tears that came unbidden. Then there was a sound of metal rolling over the pavement. The coach for Louvain had arrived. The coachman saw the young religious and stopped the horses so that he could get on.

"'Now, then, it's good-bye,' said his mother.

"Damien embraced her and climbed into the coach. As the horses went off at a fast trot, he waved his hand until he was lost to sight.

"Our hearts were crushed under our sorrow at this quick leave-taking. But little by little, our spirits arose again as we recited the rosary on the return road. We thought only of praying to Mary for the young apostle who had just broken away. But how little we knew, then, of what awaited him on Molokai!"

The following day, Brother Damien was in Paris, taking his part in the exercises of a three-day retreat preached for the missionaries by the father general.

Before setting out on the long journey, Damien wrote a letter to Tremeloo in which there is more than a suspicion of callow tactlessness. Did he have to choose that moment to sermonize, and to call up before the eyes of his kin the picture of that "stormy sea all ready to swallow" him on which he was about to sail? In later years, when life had taught him more lessons and he had seen and tasted suffering, he would be more simple and kindly. But now he wrote:

"Here we are, dear parents, at the point of leaving all that is most dear, to enter upon a stormy sea ready to swallow us.... The sacrifice is heavy. But it is the voice of God that calls us to make it. Jesus Christ is with us, his missionaries; it is he who directs our steps, who preserves us from all danger, who commands the winds to be calm, the wild beasts to flee and spiritual enemies—the devil, the world and the flesh—to leave us in peace. Already his grace is effective; and though we are about to start a perilous journey, we have no fear but are happier as usual. It is not putting it too strongly to say that we joke and laugh so much that at times our sides ache."

Then there followed a bit of gratuitous sermonizing:

"Good-bye, dear parents, good-bye. Always lead a Christian life, avoid soiling your souls with any willful faults, walk the straight and narrow path. It is the last request I make....

"Good-bye! We shall meet no more here below. But our tender love for one another will always be our bond. Once more, good-bye! Heaven's blessing on your declining years! May our Lady give you a holy death!"

For a time, the "stormy sea" of which he spoke proved to be friendly enough, but as we shall see, "the world and the devil," which then caused him little alarm, would not spare him in the years to come—indeed, would hound him fiercely to his grave.

On Thursday, October 29, the little band left Picpus and at nine o'clock in the morning boarded a train for Bremerhaven, in

Germany, where their ship awaited them. In the band were a priest, Father Christian; three clerical students; two lay brothers and ten sisters.

Before embarking, Brother Damien had his picture taken with a large crucifix in his hand, in a pose as near he could manage to the picture of Xavier at Louvain. He sent this apostolic photograph to his parents along with such meditations and exhortations as we can well imagine.

On November 2, the missionaries set foot on the *R.W. Wood*, a beautiful three-master flying the Hawaiian flag.

In addition to the sixteen members of the crew, they found on board Captain Geerken, his wife and his cousin. All were German Protestants. From the very first day, at the captain's invitation, the sons of Picpus dined at his table; and from the first, also, an excellent rapport was maintained between the religious and the crew. Damien had met his first non-Catholics, and it is surprising that he did not take them in hand to attempt their conversion by preaching the treatise "On the True Religion."

In the 1860's a journey from Paris to Honolulu by boat required four to five months or more, according to the mood of the seas and the clemency of the winds. Barring unforeseen accidents, the missionaries' voyage would not be broken by putting in at any port. From her German harbor, the *R.W. Wood* was to cut across the North Sea, traverse the Atlantic from northeast to southwest, round Cape Horn at the apex of South America, and then on the final leg sail up the Pacific toward Hawaii.

The captain reassured his passengers by telling them that every year for eight years he had made the same voyage without mishap, certainly without shipwreck. In a confident mood, then, the little community set about organizing itself for the long trip. They were lodged in cabins with bunks; they were also given two larger salons suitable for religious exercises, one for the clerics and the other for the sisters. A detailed schedule was drawn up, providing regular times for Mass, prayers, study, manual labor and recreation. Quite properly, authority was lodged in Father Christian, from whom all permissions had to be sought. But in this last arrangement, they had reckoned without thought of seasickness to which, more than all the rest, this father superior turned out to be subject. Never before was religious authority rendered so helpless.

Journal of the Voyage

The noteworthy events of the voyage are known to us through the journal of Father Christian and some letters of Brother Damien. Here is a roughly chronological account, with Damien's comments indicated by quote marks:

The ship left port on November 2, 1863. Scarcely had the tug towed the sailing vessel outside the harbor when a violent wind arose, forcing the sailors to drop anchor. After the squall, a perfect calm rendered it impossible for the vessel to move out to sea. For seven days she remained at anchor, during which the community settled down to the observance of its religious rule.

On November 9, the three-master dropped the coast below the horizon and steered into the North Sea. "We felt a frightful malaise," wrote Damien. "Our stomachs suffered from unfamiliar distress. Poor Father Christian gave up all he had swallowed; he vomited without relief and hiccuped as though his chest were going to split. His ordeal lasted a month; nor was Brother Aymard much better off."

Toward noon on November 12, they neared the English Channel. "In a few hours a violent wind drove us abreast of Dover. If it had kept up, we should have reached the Atlantic in less than three days. Unfortunately, however, up to the end of November we were checked by contrary winds. The ship had to tack back and forth, with a forward progress of only about six miles a day. For a whole month we could not have Holy Mass."

Less subject to seasickness than the others, Damien had taken on himself all the roles left vacant by the helpless sick men. He was, at various hours, sacristan, *econome* and infirmarian, without neglecting his studies in theology, which were to be continued for the duration of the voyage. At times, he even gave a helping hand to the sailors, who much preferred his muscles to his apologetics.

As sacristan, he devised a way of preventing stormy seas from tipping the chalice during Mass; and with the help of some blacking-box tops he succeeded in baking some quite acceptable hosts for the Eucharist.

As *econome*, he found that the Picpus Sisters could lend a hand. His own departure had been so hasty that his wardrobe left much to be desired. The wardrobes of certain of his confreres also needed improvement. He therefore set the sisters to work on them. Cassocks, shirts, socks and handkerchiefs passed under their competent fingers, and at the journey's end, the outfits of the Picpus men were in prime condition.

In the spirit of give and take, the clerics reciprocated for this material assistance by exercising their spiritual functions. On November 27, there was to be the renewal of religious vows. The sisters wished to prepare for it by three days of recollection. Father Christian agreed to the drawing up of a schedule. Not satisfied with this, the zealous retreatants begged him to give them several conferences each day of the retreat. Even though quite ill from seasickness, the plucky priest gave the sisters their conferences, hiccuping his way through them all.

December 1 brought a change of weather. The trade winds began to carry the ship forward at full speed. On December 22, the equator was crossed with the traditional ceremonies. By paying a forfeit to the sailors, the religious escaped the practical joking. They were not immersed in a tank and tossed across the symbolic line. It was simply as spectators that they assisted at the "baptism of the line."

The vigil of Christmas was solemnized by the vespers of the feast and chanted alternately by the men in one choir and the sisters in the other. Midnight Mass was held between matins and lauds. At seven o'clock in the morning the second and third Masses began. In the course of the day, Christmas hymns were sung, but the sisters, shy in the presence of the non-Catholic sailors, did not dare to raise their voices.

"On the first day of the new year, wrote Damien, "we sailed into sunshine.... In these waters the crew captured some magnificent specimens of albatross, which were later stuffed, some sharks,...some dolphins and some porpoises weighing as much as three hundred pounds. After that, we had five days of fine weather, then two weeks of bad."

January 19 found the ship in the treacherous Cape Horn area. She passed the very spot where, twenty years before, the *Marie-Joseph* had been wrecked, taking down to a watery death twenty-five Picpus missionaries (eight fathers, seven brothers and ten sisters), whom Bishop Rouchouze was bringing to Hawaii. "We, their successors, recited for their souls the Office of the Dead and two Rosaries."

On January 21, the ship entered the Straits of Maire. "From the first, everyone was astonished to find it so calm at Cape Horn. Some were quick to say that these parts did not deserve their bad reputation. Certainly, two days of good weather had brought us out of the dangerous straits into the Pacific. But on the very next day, a furious wind arose and drove us six hundred miles to the south. For six long days, our ship was a toy tossed about by an angry sea. We went through a veritable purgatory."

On February 2, Purification Day, "at the close of a novena, the Virgin came to our aid. The wind changed and blew strongly in the opposite direction, driving us at top speed toward the Hawaiian Islands. We still had about 7,000 miles to cover."

On February 5, "we encountered a frightful storm. In the middle of the night, the ship was battered by a raging squall which, nevertheless, drove us in the right direction. The prudent captain had had the foresight to reef his sails earlier; otherwise, the mast would have snapped. The wind blew so violently as to drive us forward at ten miles an hour, even through towering mountains of water. The heavy sailing ship pitched about like a fishing-smack. The waves smashed against her starboard side with the impact of bursting shells. The ship leaned over her beam-ends on the left, only to swing a full semicircle back to roll into the deep on her right. All through one day that dreadful rocking lasted. One had to cling like a limpet to any handy surface to avoid being hurled into the sea."

Later, Damien wrote: "After that terrible day had passed, we met only fine weather. The farther northward we advanced, the milder it became. Favorable trade winds were with us right up to Honolulu. The sky was for the most part serene, and our evenings were delightful."

At an average speed of eight miles an hour, the ship passed the shores in turn of Patagonia, Argentina, Bolivia and Peru. She crossed the equator for the second time, with everything getting better as she progressed. Then the distant shores of Panama, Costa Rica and Guatemala were passed in their turn.

The weather was fine and spirits brightened with the prospect of a not so distant landing. All the passengers forgot the hours of past anguish. "I have a very cheerful voyage," wrote Sister Mary Stanislas. "Never have I laughed so much as on the sea." The journal of Father Christian also records that all had gone well. "Joy has marked our trip," said he. "How often has laughter revealed our merry spirits. There has been no trouble from the crew, whom our firm captain has kept in hand."

In this same journal there was frequent praise of Brother Damien. Many of the entries tell of his dependability, his love of work and of prayer, his desire to be of service and his skill in getting people out of difficulties. Already he had given evidence of his strong personality. It was at this point, lest perhaps he spoil the young man, that Father Christian added: "But why speak only of him, as if everyone had not shown merit?"

The Hawaiian Archipelago was in sight. The island of Hawaii itself had been passed during the night. The ship was at that time off Maui. Soon a small island rose above the horizon and cut the blue sky with its jagged, mauve hills. It was Molokai, the island Father Damien was to make forever famous.

Chapter 4

The Hawaiian Islands

The reader might like to learn something about the people with whom Damien was casting his lot—their history, customs and way of life.

Stretching across the Pacific for almost 1,700 miles, the Hawaiian archipelago is composed of a dozen islands, of which the principal, ranging from north to south, are: Niihau, Kauai, Oahu, Molokai, Maui and Hawaii. Since Hawaii is the largest of them all, it has given its name to the group. However, the capital city, Honolulu, lies on the island of Oahu.

Composed chiefly of basalt and lava, and ringed about by coral reefs, the Hawaiian Islands are the tips of steep-sloped volcanic mountains. Originally the islands were barren. In the course of ages, however, the valleys and parts of the hillsides became covered with a thick deposit of marvelously fertile soil which nourishes eucalyptus and orange trees, the banana plant, the coconut palm and the laurel rose, as well as ferns, trees with blood-red branches and creeping vines with leaves and flowers of varied shapes and colors. The climate is dry and the temperature moderate. The heat is kept from being oppressive by the spicy breeze that blows incessantly.

The Kanakas

It seems hardly credible that so mild a land should have been peopled by cruel and bloodthirsty natives. Yet, native Kanakas bore an evil reputation that dated from February 14, 1779, the day when they fell upon the explorer Cook and his crewmen and massacred them just a year after their first landing.

When the Englishmen had first arrived, they had received an open-hearted welcome. The native priests had acclaimed Cook himself as an ancient god returning to his land after a long voyage. With ceremony, the chieftains had also come to him and offered him all the assistance in their power. The people prostrated themselves before him, giving him symbolic gifts of fruit. Never before in their exploration of the Pacific had these sailors received such honor. The pleased captain named the islands after his patron, the Earl of Sandwich.

Did the explorers abuse this rare hospitality? Many writers believe they did. Resentment became hot when, in order to get some firewood, Cook ordered his men to demolish a temple and carry aboard ship its wooden furnishings, including some idols. Brawls between sailors and natives became frequent. On Sunday, February 14, when Cook and his crews went ashore to seize an uncooperative chief, they were met and surrounded by natives armed with clubs, who beat the explorers so ruthlessly that they perished to a man.

For many years thereafter, navigators and merchant seamen had little stomach for putting in at the Sandwich Islands.

It is not our intention to picture the Kanakas as history shows them, defending their hearths and homes in the early years of European explorations or later succumbing to some of the evil influences brought in by white colonists. For our purposes it is enough to describe them as they were in earlier centuries and as they were generally found to be during the years when Damien knew them.

The race was handsome and muscular. The men often resembled bronze statues; the women had beautiful eyes and in their youth were well-proportioned and graceful.

If occasion had found the Kanakas to be combative and even cruel, they were ordinarily peaceful, gentle and hospitable — intelligent and poetic by instinct. They were also inclined to indolence, a trait that met no rebuke from the prolific and generous world that surrounded them. Nature unrolled a charming panorama before their eyes and, without requiring them to exert themselves too much, furnished them with all they needed for life.

The native hut was made of large leaves interwoven with long grasses. These were propped against the trunk of a tree, whose lower branches were used as roof-beams, bound to one another by ropes made from pliant plants. Not a single nail was used. Inside the hut, rushes were strewn over the ground from wall to wall, and in one corner were stored the kitchen utensils, which consisted of a large gourd and several smaller ones. Upon the walls hung fishing-lines, fish hooks fashioned from bones, spears, a bow with arrows and a heavy club. Outside, a shed of palm leaves sheltered an outrigger canoe with its paddles, as well as a mortar for grating taro roots.

Taro, from which was made a kind of paste called poi, was the basic food of the Kanakas. They might garnish it with some sweet potatoes, or fresh shrimps, or the flesh of a suckling pig that had been stewed in a covered pot set in a trench filled with heated stones, or with various kinds of fish or with the fruits that grew so prolifically. People sat on the ground to eat, without benefit of table or knives or forks; they drank water or "awa," an alcoholic drink of which they were passionately fond.

After the meal, the men smoked their pipes while telling and retelling stories that never ended. On feast days the women and girls chanted love poems to the accompaniment of guitars, or with flowers twined into their hair danced until exhausted. It should be noted that feast days were very common in this land, and that even on ordinary days, the great affair of life was pleasure. Manners were complacent and morals lax.

Hawaiians have never been cannibals. Nevertheless, in order to placate a god, human sacrifices were sometimes offered—with the victim chosen from among prisoners of war or condemned criminals.

Women were never led to the altar of sacrifice, yet they were not considered the equals of men. They did not eat with the men, nor did they take a place in a canoe. By way of exception, a noblewoman was allowed to ascend the throne and rule a tribe, and it was through the women in the family that the noble line descended.

People who have borrowed Hawaiian dances and music, could also imitate the Kanakas in other ways. The Hawaiians loved the noble, the beautiful and the sublime; they had an instinct for justice; they manifested their loyalty and affection in charming ways. The chiefs, in particular, had a sense of honor that impelled them to respect their pledged word and to come to the aid of friends even at the risk of life itself.

The chiefs (*Alii*) were the rulers; the sorcerers (*Kahumas*) were the doctors; the ordinary people (*Makaai nana*) were merely subjects without right of appeal.

The ancient history of Hawaii was largely a series of songs and tales celebrating the varying fortunes of the chiefs as they formed alliances with one another; or warred one upon another; or toppled thrones and destroyed the occupants; or enlarged their territories by annexing someone else's; or suffered in their turn spoliation and defeat. When fortune smiled, a chief became king of an entire island, and even of an archipelago. He had an army and held as his property both land and people. He meted out justice and punished lawbreakers. He requisitioned vegetables, fruit, fish, fiber-cloth and fishing nets, as well as the yellow and red feathers with which he liked to adorn his royal mantle.

The law he enforced was the law of the *taboo*. Taboo embraced many detailed directives which had to be observed under pain of death or mutilation. It forbade allowing one's shadow to fall on the person of a chief, or pronouncing his name in song. It barred women from eating bananas, coconut meat, pork, or chicken, since these items of food were reserved for the gods and for men. People could be put to death for the crime of coughing, sneezing or making some other noise during the religious rites.

The official interpretation of taboos was the prerogative of the sorcerers. These latter were usually astute men who knew how to keep the common people subservient to their rulers. They read the significance of movements in the skies and in the sea; they divined the intentions of the gods and had the power of appeasing divine displeasure; they were expert in using medicinal plants to cure diseases; they quieted disturbed minds; they preached respect for established authority; and they transmitted from father to son their secret knowledge and their prerogatives.

These sorcerers wielded great power; for the Kanakas were religious even to the point of credulity. They had a confused belief in a Creator who made the first man and who rewarded or punished every person according to his works: the good being transported to some beautiful island of cool shade under coconut trees; the wicked being thrown through a gaping crater leading to the land of the evil spirits where all was dark and icy cold.

The Hawaiian had a special belief in malignant gods inhabiting the earth, the sea and the air. He attributed to them all the calamities he suffered. In his eyes, volcanoes, thunder, earthquakes, hurricanes, sickness and all the unmastered forces of nature were the works of preternatural beings whose anger had to be appeased. The most terrible of them were Pele and Maui, who around 1820 were reported as making a new demand for human sacrifice. The goddess Pele directed the activity of volcanoes, while Maui specialized in pushing islands up from the depths of the sea, procuring fire for men and keeping the sun in hand, lest it move too fast or wobble from its orbit.

Hawaiian History

A great deal is known about the civil and religious history of Hawaii under the rule of five kings, the last three of whom were contemporaries of Damien.

Kamehameha I ruled from 1784 to 1819. In their admiration, his subjects called him "the Napoleon of the Pacific."

His authority was at first limited to the island of Hawaii, but soon it was extended to the whole archipelago, bringing order and prosperity to every district. This king was politically astute and not reluctant to utilize the resources of foreigners. After having forcibly detained two American sailors, Isaac Davis and John Young, the king prevailed upon them to assist him. He was also skillful enough to get the collaboration of the navigator Vancouver, who imported sheep and cattle into the kingdom, taught its ruler the principles of foreign politics and introduced him to the craft of shipbuilding.

In his eighty-second year, Kamehameha forbade the human sacrifice his people wished to offer to obtain a longer life for him. He took the opportunity to designate his son Liholiko as his successor and to prescribe by law that the most intelligent of his favorites, Kaahumanu, was to exercise royal power jointly with his son.

The wisdom of this latter precaution was clear from the moment the son ascended the throne under the name of Kamehameha II: he was notably lacking in responsibility. Dropping the experienced friends of his father, he surrounded himself with second-rate advisers; he admitted foreigners without restriction; and by giving himself to pleasure and debauchery and draining the public treasury, he gave his subordinate chieftains a detestable example they were not slow to follow. He had no fewer than five wives at one time. Under his rule the taboo was abolished, temples were demolished and the sorcerers fled to the hills. Thus, the field was opened for the planting of new religions.

Protestantism entered this field when some American Presbyterian missionaries and their families landed at Honolulu in 1820: two ministers, a farmer, a doctor, a mechanic, a catechist and a printer. They were given complete freedom of activity by the king and in consequence soon achieved a commanding position in the realm.

The Protestant ministers had an initial piece of good fortune. They baptized a six-foot native woman of great local influence. With the ardent zeal of the convert, this amazon proceeded to offer insult to the goddess Pele in her mountain home. She gravely walked across the field of lava which lay between Pele's volcano and the crowd of terrified spectators and hurled branches and fruit into the crater, defying the goddess to come forth and take revenge for the sacrilege. The crowd expected the blasphemer to be struck down by lightning. But nothing of the sort happened. The woman turned toward the people and shouted: "You now see clearly that Pele is powerless. She has not dared to take up my challenge. Believe me: there is only one God, who is Jehovah, and only one Savior, who is Jesus Christ Our Lord!" After she had spoken, the Kanakas present were converted; and when many who had not been there heard of what had passed, they, too, presented themselves for baptism.

Thus, the Presbyterians succeeded in planting themselves solidly among the Hawaiians. Presbyterianism became to a large extent the state religion and gave its adherents an advantage from which they were quick to profit.

Kamehameha II, who had been following his desire to visit foreign lands, died of measles in London in 1824. He had reigned five years.

Under his successor, Kamehameha III, Catholics made their first apostolic efforts. On July 7, 1827, six French Picpus Fathers came to Hawaii and were quite well received. It was not long before they made some converts. In addition to their personal witness, they brought a religion that appealed to the Kanaka temperament and, as far as possible, respected local customs.

Unfortunately, their progress was soon slowed down. During the twenty-nine-year rule of Kamehameha III, the non-Catholic missionaries maintained their ascendancy. As for the Picpus Fathers, by royal ordinance they were thrown into a small boat and dropped on a section of the California coast far from any habitation.

In 1835, an Irish catechist risked his life to go to the missionaries' shepherdless flocks. Since he was a subject of the King of England, the authorities closed their eyes to this audacious foreigner. The next year, another Irishman, a Picpus Father named Walsh, also put his life in jeopardy; he was likewise ignored. This apparent tolerance by the government encouraged the Picpus deportees to return from California the following year. However, they were arrested, and it took a demonstration by French and British warships to affect their release. Their freedom was short-lived, however; as soon as the French frigate and English corvette had departed, the missionaries were once again harassed and forced to quit the Islands. This time they took refuge in Chile.

Two years passed, during which Catholic Kanakas, left to themselves, practiced their religion in secret. At times they were faithful to the point of heroism.

There came a day, however, when the French took the matter in hand and sent the frigate *Artemise* with her sixty cannon to drop anchor in the harbor of Honolulu. It was July 9, 1839. Nothing more was needed to bring Kamehameha to terms, including the payment of 100,000 francs to the French government by way of reparation. A favorable customs treaty and guarantees protecting the religious rights of French nationals were also conceded. In the following years, the king was led to proclaim religious freedom and to establish a parliament.

The legal foundation of the Picpus missions in Hawaii dates from this period. On May 14, 1840, Bishop Rouchouze arrived with some confreres. Finding that the Catholic numbered about 2,000, the bishop judged that the size of his vineyard called for more laborers. He hastened back to France to fetch them. The joy of returning from his successful quest was quenched in the cold waters near Cape Horn when the shipwreck we mentioned earlier took to the bottom the bishop and the twenty-four missionaries who were accompanying him to Hawaii.

As with soldiers on the battlefield, so it is with apostles of the Gospel. When one falls, others rush to take his place in the combat. That disaster did not dampen the zeal of the Picpus Fathers, nor did it retard the progress of their mission. In 1845, soon after the death of Bishop Rouchouze, the Pope raised the archipelago to the status of Vicariate Apostolic and placed Bishop Maigret at its head. There were now 13,000 Catholics among the Hawaiians, but the number was to be trebled under the reign of Kamehameha IV (1855-1863). This king had great respect for Bishop Maigret and invited him to bring in some Picpus sisters for the education of girls. Ten sisters arrived in 1859. By adding their number to the eighteen priests and twelve catechists already there, they brought to forty the total of men and women who were laboring in this mission field when Damien came to join them.

After Kamehameha IV died, his successor, Kamehameha V, began a reign which lasted from 1863 to 1872. He favored the immigration of foreigners and modernized the apparatus of administration. To advance this policy, he attached to himself as prime minister and general factotum the distinguished Frenchman, M. de Varigny, a writer for the *Revue des Deux Mondes*.

With the death of this king, the dynasty of the Kamehamehas came to its end.

Lunalilo, successor of Kamehameha V, ruled only thirteen months and grew from day to day more helpless in the face of maneuvers for influence on the part of France, the United States and England.

In 1874, Kalakaua mounted the throne with the blessing of the United States. Seventeen years later he died at the Palace hotel in San Francisco—the victim, rumor had it, of overindulgence in dainty food.

During the last fifteen years of his life, Kalakaua was a constitutional monarch who enjoyed few powers of governing. After his death, his remains were enbalmed, placed in a crystal coffin and brought on a warship from San Francisco to Honolulu, where his body lay in state for fifteen days.

Kalakaua was succeeded by his sister, Liliuokalani, who yielded to popular desires and tried to restore her country's independence. But the United States had friends in the palace. In 1893, the warship *Boston* dropped anchor at Honolulu. Protected by her guns, these friends dethroned the ruler, proclaimed a republic and asked to be annexed by the United States.

Responsible opinion regarded this proposal as contrary to the Monroe Doctrine. In 1898, however, the Hawaiian Islands were seen as necessary for national defense, and, since the people of the Islands seemed to desire the transfer, the archipelago was annexed in that same year. Two years later, Hawaii became a U.S. territory. In 1959, the Islands were admitted as the fiftieth state.

When Captain Cook landed in Hawaii, he calculated that the Kanakas numbered 400,000, but there may have been only half as many. In 1832 the number was 130,000, and at the time of Father Damien, there were about 60,000. Today the Kanakas have all but disappeared.

Chapter 5

The District of Puna

Brother Damien landed at Honolulu on the morning of March 19, 1864. The next day he wrote to his family: "The arrival of the missionaries and of the six sisters all dressed in white made a deep impression on the crowds that came flocking from every direction. They escorted us to the cathedral, which was already thronged. Father Christian celebrated Holy Mass, which was followed by the singing of the *Te Deum*. I was much surprised to find so beautiful a church in the Hawaiian Islands. It is 175 feet long by 50 feet wide.

"The rest of that day and all the next we spent exchanging handclasps. I think I grasped more than a thousand outstretched hands. Bishop Louis Maigret, who has been wearing himself out here for thirty years, sang a High Mass and preached in Kanaka. The bishop and Father Modeste, the provincial, are goodness and simplicity personified."

Without going into a detailed explanation, we note here that the mission had at its head two persons with roles theoretically distinct: Bishop Maigret and the provincial, Father Modeste. Both resided in Honolulu and both were members of the Picpus Congregation. The first, with his authority stemming directly from the Holy See in Rome, had jurisdiction over the religious in so far as they were missionaries; the second, holding his power from Picpus, had jurisdiction over the missionaries in so far as they were religious. Clearly these two divisions overlapped and were bound to give occasion for differences of opinion.

Ordination

On the vigil of Easter, March 26, Brother Damien was ordained a sub-deacon, and immediately thereafter he was sent to the College of Ahuimanu, where he remained for two months in preparation for the priesthood. Against the background of a countryside littered with huge rocks and furrowed by deep gorges, he finished his seminary studies and made his final retreat before ordination. He had completed his studies at a remarkable rate, covering in four years what others did in ten! Of course, his powers of assimilation were unusually strong, and the bishop was anxious to make prompt use of the recruits that the *R.W. Wood* had brought him.

It was in Honolulu on May 21 that Damien was raised to the priesthood, together with Brother Clement, his companion on the voyage. At the ceremony were throngs of Catholics from all the islands, who had come to see the young spiritual fathers they had so fervently desired. Wrote Damien: "I feared my heart would melt like wax when for the first time I distributed to them the Bread of Life."

Very humbly and a little solemnly he added: "Here I am, dear Parents, a missionary in a land that is corrupt, heretical and idolatrous. How serious are my obligations! How great must be my apostolic zeal! What a pure heart, what a sound mind, what a prudent judgment must be mine henceforth! Alas! how shall I, who so often in the past have grieved you by my fickleness, rise to be equal to such obligations? I beg you not to forget the poor priest who day and night will be tramping about the volcanoes of the Sandwich Islands in search of stray sheep. Pray to God for me day and night; have prayers said for me; for, if God should withdraw his grace from me, I myself should quickly fall into the very mire from which I wish to draw others. Farewell, dear Parents!"

And for the first time he signed himself: "J. Damien de Veuster, Missionary Priest." Henceforth, he would be known as *Father Damien.*

Bishop Maigret assigned him, as well as Father Clement, a district each on the Island of Hawaii as the field for their apostolate. He wished to have his new missionaries near at hand so as to watch over their first efforts.

One evening in June, all three took ship at Honolulu. On the morning of the next day, their boat stopped at Maui. They took advantage of the opportunity to go ashore and say Mass. By good fortune, they found at home their three confreres who lived there: Fathers Aubert, Gregory and Leonor.

Damien would have liked to delay among them, but scarcely had their Masses been finished when the boat whistle blew and it was necessary to go aboard again. "It cost me a great deal to leave our confreres so soon without knowing whether I should ever see them again. I complained to the good God, asking him to give me the privilege of spending some days with them so as to profit from their experience. The advice of veterans is very useful for a young missionary. Even if one had learned by heart all the books of theology, he would still not know how to put them into practice."

Scarcely had the passengers re-embarked when they were obliged to return ashore. At the very moment of departure, fire had been discovered in the hold. Soon it spread to the hull. The missionaries had to wait for another ship.

The bishop was pressed for time, having a chapel to bless on the Island of Hawaii on the Feast of Sts. Peter and Paul.

Father Damien, however, gave thanks to God for the opportunity to study Kanaka with Father Aubert. He was also eager to try his new powers, and he asked permission to go to evangelize some Christians who were living eighteen miles from there. Out of fear that a ship might arrive during his absence, the bishop hesitated to agree; finally, however, he yielded to the young man's earnest request.

It is not surprising that the first sermon of the new apostle should appear labored. Although he knew quite well what he wanted to say, he found difficulty in saying it in Kanaka. At times he was at a total loss for the proper word. To tide him over, he would draw his large handkerchief from his pocket and proceed to mop his face until some appropriate word came back to him. The Kanakas themselves made allowance for his untrained tongue and were quite satisfied with the sermon.

On his return to the mission, the young preacher discovered that in the meantime the bishop and Father Clement had taken passage toward their destination. Profiting by this new delay, Damien set out again on a circuit of the island and spent several more days among the Kanakas under the June sun. Once the damage wrought by the fire had been repaired, he sailed to rejoin his companions.

He had counted on meeting the bishop at the newly dedicated chapel, but learned that Maigret had not waited for him there. By this time, he was at the other end of the island, 180 miles away, on a pastoral visitation. Over hill and through valley, sometimes on foot and sometimes on horse, Damien went in search of the bishop, and finally caught up with him on July 24. Four days later, fortified by the final instructions of his shepherd, he went to the place his heart was set on: the district of Puna.

"The Big Island"

The island of Hawaii, where Damien was to spend a third of his apostolic career, is divided into six districts: Kohala, Kona, Hau, Puna, Hamakua and Hilo. It is the largest of the Hawaiian Islands. Its surface constitutes almost two-thirds of the land area of the whole archipelago. Its shoreline extends for about 400 miles. Snow-capped mountains, some of them 12,000 feet in height, alternate with fertile valleys and virgin forests. Here and there black streams of cooled lava have pierced through the central ridges of the island and descended into the sea.

Hawaii is preeminently the land of the volcano. In no other part of the world are volcanoes so numerous or so formidable. The most extraordinary is Kilauea, which has no fewer than a thousand craters. It lies squarely on the border of Puna. Imagine a circle about nine miles in circumference around which rise walls 600 feet high. This circle encloses Halemaumau, the so-called home of Pele, the "goddess" of eternal fire.

The appearance of Halemaumau is always changing: the width and depth and shape of its lava are never the same. "At this moment," wrote a traveler who visited the spot in 1892, "there is a circular well about 60 feet deep and 300 feet in diameter full of incandescent lava always bubbling and gurgling, from which emerge jets of flame thirty feet high and billows of fire which break upon the crater's rim. From the indescribably intense heat and boiling and bubbling of this hellish blast-furnace, one is continually turning one's face for relief; but one's eyes are always drawn back again to follow the course of the ever-surging flames. Stone, in the process of melting, leaps crackling from depths of the earth, explodes and falls back again into the cauldron. The spectacle induces a nervous dread and a giddiness more appalling than that caused by a vast void.... Some of the liquid lava thrown into the air is rarefied somewhat by the action of the wind and drops back like fireworks in long, silky filaments as of spun glass golden in color: the hair of the goddess Pele, say the Kanakas."

Many writers have praised the variety of the Hawaiian landscape. It would be difficult to pile up more expressions of appreciation than those used by them to convey their admiration. But we should not look for similar enthusiasm in the letters of Father Damien. He was not an artist, nor did he have that Franciscan cast of mind which finds in nature unending occasion for raising one's heart in praise of the goodness of God.

On a visit to Kilauea, he remarked: "There's nothing here worth seeing, except the action caused by fire of intense heat before which even mountains melt." Then passing on to his real interest, he added: "When it goes into action, our poor islanders are terrified, and many of them run to offer sacrifice in appeasement. I myself witnessed such idolatry on a day when I was descending into the interior of the volcano. A Kanaka was in the very act of sacrificing to the goddess. I took the opportunity to give him a little sermon on hell."

In an effort to remove all illusion from the mind of his young co-worker, Bishop Maigret recalled for him the words of the Savior about those who gather without having sown and those who sow without hope of ever gathering.

There was in sober truth no harvest to gather at Puna when Damien set to work there. In that vast district which took three days to cross, there were 350 Catholics scattered among non-Catholics and pagans. They had neither school nor church, and indeed they had had no resident priest for seven years. Under the circumstances, it is hardly surprising that the faith had found it difficult to survive. The faithful had become as lax in their habits as the other Kanakas. "The laws of the land scarcely encourage the stability of the marriage bond," sighed Damien. But immorality is to be found in all countries at all times, and it does not keep an apostle from preaching the Kingdom of God to the poor.

As a man of action who could always find in hope reasons to justify his action, he made allowance for extenuating circumstances and said optimistically: "With energy and good habits, these people would be excellent."

He then lost no time in praising the inhabitants, whom he already loved as his children: "These people are gentle, affable and full of generous impulses. They have neither desire for wealth nor love of luxury. They would deprive themselves of necessities in order to provide for a guest. Even the non-Catholics give a hearty welcome to the priest when he goes among them. I have yet to be insulted by them."

Who would have dreamed of insulting a man so appealing to the tastes of the natives? Damien had a handsome and manly face, the strength of Hercules, a soft and sonorous voice (marvelously suited to the Kanaka language, in which vowels abound), pleasing manners, hearty good humor and a disinterested devotion that seemed inexhaustible. Everyone was drawn to him.

"Our poor Islanders are very happy when they see *Kamiano* (the Kanaka name for Damien) coming, and I, for my part, love them very dearly; I would gladly give my life for them. I do not spare myself when it is necessary to go on a sick-call that takes me twenty to twenty-five miles away. Ordinarily, I make such trips on horseback without great fatigue. As for Kanaka, I already know enough of it to preach, to hear confessions and to carry on discussions with non-Catholics. All things considered, I am very happy, for, along with all the privations and hardships, God often gives me consolations beyond all expectations."

His ministry consisted in scouring, in every sense of the word, a parish that was as large as a province, in preaching, hearing confessions, baptizing, visiting the sick, recruiting neophytes and preparing the dying. "His zeal did not allow him to remain more than a day in any one place," said his co-worker in that field.

It is no exaggeration to say that in his mission everything had to be rebuilt from the ground up. There was no chapel, since the old one had crumbled away. At first he said Mass in native huts. Then he built some "prayer houses" from what material was at hand. He raised no fewer than six of them in eight months. They were only poor huts, but until better could be provided, they served the religious needs of such small flocks as he managed to gather.

All this activity wreaked havoc on his religious lifestyle. "Here, in place of the hidden life, there are endless trips by land or by sea, on foot or on horseback; instead of observing silence, one has constantly to speak with all sorts of people; instead of being directed, one must direct others. The most difficult task of all, in the midst of so many vexations, is to maintain a spirit of recollection and of prayer."

The superior general, to whom Damien directed this self-criticism, had no need to be concerned about a son who himself was worried about this matter. Far from relaxing in his quest for self-improvement, this young man aimed at perfecting himself, and he humbly begged his correspondents to seek for him graces of which he believed himself unworthy: "If Providence had sent here a Cure d'Ars, the lost sheep would quickly return to the fold.... O my dear brother, pray yourself and get many others to pray that your poor brother may not yield to temptations, that his words may carry the persuasiveness of the Holy Spirit."

If he seemed to be gaining some success in his apostolate, he credited it to God and to the prayers of others: "I consider myself an instrument in the hands of God. How many times in these last months have I been providentially led aside from my appointed road to enter little cabins where I had the opportunity of reconciling with God old persons on the threshold of eternity!"

The Kanaka language mastered, six chapels built, general good-will won, several baptisms administered, some sinners converted at the last moment: such were his achievements when, at the end of eight months, Damien left his first mission. His going can be attributed to the unsatisfactory health of Father Clement, who was the pastor of Kohala and Kamakua, two districts bordering on Damien's own.

By dint of traveling some hundred miles toward a central point, these two religious were able to meet at lengthy intervals. In the course of one such meeting in January, 1865, Father Clement voiced his discontent. The vast territory in his charge made demands on him that were beyond his strength. Full of rocks, gorges and precipices, innocent of roads and indeed even of paths in some quarters, that district called for a robust man who could handle a horse well and surmount all the obstacles in his way. Father Clement remarked that his confrere was much better equipped than he for the mission of Kohala; and he proposed an exchange of districts, subject to the bishop's approval. Damien accepted the proposal at once, and the bishop agreed that there were good reasons for the change. Thus it was that, on March 19, 1865, Father Damien took the road leading to Kohala, where he was to remain for eight years.

When he wrote to inform Pamphile of the transfer, he confessed: "So close had my dear Christians become to my heart, that the separation from them was more difficult to bear than parting from our dear parents had been."

Chapter 6

The District of Kohala

Father Damien's new parish of 3,000 persons was about 80 miles long and about 30 miles wide. "I devoted a full month to touring it," he wrote. For five years it had been without a pastor – until Father Clement's arrival.

He actually gave six weeks to his inspection, learning to his sorrow that "brambles and thornbushes crowded out the good grain. Yet, there did remain a few faithful souls, almost lost among heretics and idolators." One wooden church also had remained standing. It had three altars, three chandeliers trimmed with artificial flowers and a bell. There was also a priest-house made of *pala* leaves; it was still quite usable.

The program of the new pastor was quickly drawn up. He would devote himself to the spiritual needs of his flock to the limit of his strength, leaving it to the divine will to quicken his field for the harvest or to leave his seedplot apparently sterile. "It is for the Master of the vineyard to give the increase. The missionary is only the humble workman who plants and waters. Sometimes the vine grows; sometimes it withers. But I know that if one fails to plant, nothing grows but thorns."

The method he followed in his apostolate sprang from the

example given by his Divine Master in his dealings with his fellow men. "I love my Kanakas very much," he wrote, "and I do all I can for them. On their part, they love me as children love father and mother. It is from this mutual affection, I hope, that their conversion will come. Ah! dear sister, how I love my simple people!"

Life in the Saddle

Most of the time he was on the road, exercising his zeal and spending his strength. To a Kanaka who asked, "Where is your house?" he replied: "Here!" and pointed to the saddle on his horse.

"On our trips," he wrote, "we use mules and horses. I have just bought, in a fair deal, a fine horse for 100 francs and a mule for 75. Sometimes I must learn to travel in a canoe."

Two years later, the price had dropped by a half. Perhaps he had learned to keep his eyes peeled, for he wrote: "I always have mules and horses. They cost 25 to 50 francs."

Though his mounts were excellent, they did not always succeed in getting him where he wanted to go. Fortunately, he was a good climber and was quite capable of teaching mountaineering to his natives.

"One village in my mission might be the most inaccessible in the entire archipelago. The path leading to it is so dangerous as to be impassable even on mule-back. Neither beast nor rider would return. Picture, in a stretch of twelve miles, a dozen deep ravines and just as many rocky ridges to cross. One of the peaks is 2000 feet high. What of it? I take only forty minutes to scale this peak. Of course, I am completely winded when I reach the top.

"There is another Catholic settlement with an approach almost as difficult. It can be reached only by sea. Unfortunately, the sea near it is usually in a bad mood. I tried to go there on the first Sunday in October; but I tell you, my dear Parents, that on that occasion your Joe barely escaped drowning. On Saturday morning, the sea had seemed calm enough; and your Joe went to the beach and pushed off in a Kanaka pirogue, a small boat made from a hollowed log about twelve feet long. Joe took care to make an act of contrition before stepping into it. Later, we were moving swiftly over the water when suddenly one of the paddlers cried, '*Pitikia*! We are lost!' and the pirogue turned turtle and threw your Joe and his two companions into the sea. Fortunately, your son had learned to swim in the ponds of Tremeloo. Thanks to that skill and with the help of a plank he was able to make the shore with no damage outside a water-soaked breviary."

His journeying was not too burdensome for him. "To spend six weeks on a trip is nothing for me; for, wherever I go, I am at home. Since I carry no money, I have no fear of thieves. The first house reached serves as a hotel. I find there all I need, and no one thinks of accepting any payment. As for the horses and mules, they don't cost much to feed now. When we halt for the evening, I tie them with a long rope for the night, and they browse on the grass they find within easy reach."

On some trips the unforeseen happened: "One evening as I reached the summit of a mountain, about fifteen miles from my home, my mule snapped his bit, started off at a gallop and carried me into the midst of a herd of wild cattle. I was off my track, night was falling and I was drenched and hungry. Fortunately, just then a dog barked in the distance. I moved in the direction of the barking, and found a Kanaka hut where they received me most cordially."

The Catholic community he was to visit the next day had a hundred members. "It has a schoolhouse, a sort of cabin made of straw with an entrance about four feet high through which the wind blows at will, so that Mass-candles when lit and re-lit are snuffed out again and again. When I arrive, I set up the altar: a plank resting on four stakes driven into the earthen floor. My people have been gathering all morning for confessions—without benefit of a confessional, I need not add. At nine o'clock, upon the blowing of a horn, which is merely a large shell, the faithful assemble for Mass. (In this connection, dear Parents, if you could manage to send me a bell, it would not take me long to drop that wretched horn). During the Holy Sacrifice, all the people recite aloud the Mass prayers, which they know by heart. My sermon deals with the Gospel and the great love of Jesus for us. Some of the Kanakas receive Communion. When the liturgy is finished, all go to the hut in which I passed the night and wait there to chat with me. My host has prepared for me a good fish and a kind of paste (*poi*). When my meal is over, the horn is blown once more and the faithful return to the church for Rosary, and later for catechism and finally for evening prayers. Afterwards, they come to shake my hand, and then they return contented to their huts."

Father Damien gave no place in his homilies to fine words and subtle thoughts. He went right to the point, thundering against error and vice, exhorting his people to repent and to pray, teaching them to make belief and practice agree. In a deep warm voice, he spoke in a lively and familiar manner, so that no listener went from his sermon ignorant of its meaning. Sometimes he was driven to exasperation by the incontinence of some of his flock or by the practice of magic, which some were slow in renouncing. Generally, however, his tone was encouraging and kindly.

"I had quite a number of people at Mass today. After reading the Gospel, like St. John the Baptist, I lashed out against sinners. I bore down a little too hard, I am afraid."

He had his work cut out for him in attempting to lead his Catholics to a pure life, among a people so lax, and to get them to understand that marriage is indissoluble.

"For example, this year you marry two persons. They live in peace for two or three months, then a little dispute crops up, and then you have your couple separated for good. Each of them sets up another establishment. But the civil law forbids adultery! They are brought to court and fined 150 francs. This puts them in debt for many years to come. In the long run, they will get a divorce and thereupon will enter upon another marriage. But, in that case, would the priest be able to give absolution again?"

The sorcerers gave him a great deal of trouble. He could scarcely have avoided dealing with them in his sermons as he spoke of them in his letters:

"Has a Catholic fallen ill? He summons with the help of his neighbors the doctor he thinks capable of curing him. This specialist is quickly notified. But he does not respond without deliberation. First he pauses in recollection and whispers a prayer to the god whose priest he is. Then he puts his hand into a little bag full of black and white pebbles. If he takes out a black pebble, it is useless to start out, for his god will do nothing for that client. If, on the contrary, it turns out to be white pebble, the god is favorable and the trip to the patient will be worth the sorcerer's time.

"Upon arrival, the sorcerer draws from the sick man a sort of confession which makes it clear that an unfulfilled vow is at the bottom of the trouble. By way of retaliation, the offended god has entered the body of the unfortunate man and is causing him to suffer until satisfaction has been given.... A speedy sacrifice of propitiation, then, is in order. It requires a pig that has been cooked in an oven, along with intoxicating liquors which, after first being offered to the deity involved, are distributed in turn to the priest, the sick man and the neighbors. After the rites have ended, the charlatan, who knows no more medicine than my horse, goes out into the forest and gathers herbs to be given to the sick man. Quite often the next day finds the patient dead, but the sorcerer still in full possession of his prestige.

"In connection with this meal, my dear Pamphile, what would you, a theologian, do if you had to deal in confession with Kanakas who accuse themselves of partaking of it? It should be pointed out that it is largely for the food that they go to the sick man's house...."

The Builder

Although his personal life was that of a poor man, Father Damien did have some need of money. The son of the grain-dealer of Tremeloo had not lost his business sense: "The bishop has bought me a large piece of land," he wrote; "I shall plant some coffee trees there later on. In the meantime, I have borrowed 400 francs with which I can pay my debts."

Tobacco was expensive in Hawaii, despite the fact that there was an annual yield of several crops. Damien spoke with admiration of a Belgian compatriot, a recent arrival, who made considerable money out of it. He imitated the newcomer, at least on a small scale, for we have a letter of his which announced a consignment of tobacco to Honolulu. The superior of the Picpus sisters, with whom he got along very well, was stationed there. "I am sending you," he wrote to the provincial, "some potatoes from my Catholics. Potatoes can always be used. Let her keep them, then,...and pay for them. The money will serve to settle a bill which I owe."

He kept pigs, chickens, bees and sheep. He mentioned them to Pamphile: "After having attended to the Lord's flock, Joe must busy himself with his own sheep. He bought 55 of them at 2.50 francs apiece. From time to time, one of them goes to the kitchen oven." But the others? Probably they were resold at a profit.

A series of letters has been kept in which Damien sent

orders to Honolulu for lumber, shingles, glass, locks, kilograms of nails and all kinds of materials used in construction work. All this was very accurately accounted for, and the money needed for these purchases was provided to the penny. This money often came from his Catholics, whose indolence he found ways of discouraging.

He kept an eye on his bank balance and was always aware of what was owed him: "I am in debt," he wrote to his provincial, "with a merchant in Hilo for some paint I bought. Will you not find it possible to get Father Charles to pay for it? This arrangement seems to me to be fair, for when his mule had died of hunger while waiting for him to return from Honolulu, I gave him my better mule in its place. I do not mention the many sows for which he still owes me."

It was chiefly for the building of churches that Damien needed money. "A chapel costs me fifteen hundred francs," he said in a letter.

No sooner was he installed in Kohala, than he began to beg from his bishop, who was poor enough, and from his provincial, who was scarcely less destitute. When the latter wrote to the father general about him, he called him "good Father Damien." He was happy to praise him: "Father Damien is always undaunted, for he fears nothing; he tames the most unruly mules!"

The provincial, however, could not always see eye to eye with him: "Father Damien came to see us, or rather, he came to ask that two chapels be built for him. He had scarcely given me time to look into his noble face, always frank and glowing with health.... It is easier to draw up plans than to follow them out.... I told him so. Of course, he is right in wanting to get materials to be used in building temples of the Holy Spirit, but we must proceed slowly; chapels do not grow like mushrooms."

Damien dreamed of the chapels and of the assistance they would give to the conversion of souls; he knew that nothing attracted the Kanaka to the faith more strongly than beautiful and colorful ceremonies performed in a temple where the presence of God is felt. "The pomp of our rites," he said in a letter, "has a profound effect and leads many to ask for instructions."

Since chapels did not grow like mushrooms, as his superior had put it, Damien set about making them, so to speak, spring from the earth. In this district he built eight of them with his own hands.

Perhaps a word of explanation is in order.

When a diocesan weekly in its obituary-notices congratulates a pastor on having been a "great builder," it has in mind his skill in collecting the funds needed so that masons and contractors can raise the buildings.

Father Damien played a more distinguished role. Not only was he his own architect and foreman, but he also put his own hand to the job itself, working like any laborer. We have already seen that he could act as substitute for almost any kind of workman. His herculean strength impressed the Kanakas as much as his apologetics. His bishop wrote: "The natives cry out in amazement when they see him carrying down from the mountain on his shoulder beams that they, putting every ounce of their strength to the task, would have found difficulty in lifting."

Damien has told how he went about his church building.

"Will you follow me to a place about a hundred miles from here? There had never been a church there. On my first visit, I baptized a good number of catechumens and suggested that they help me build a little chapel as an act of thanksgiving. They agreed. At once they went up into the mountain and cut some very fine trees. They then sawed them into planks, etc., according to specifications I had drawn up. I stayed on the spot and raised the framework (carpenters are highly paid here). I, therefore, did the work of construction with the help of two Kanakas, and did not do too bad a job. When I come this way again, I shall give the finishing touches to the interior and I shall raise over the front the large cross for which the Kanakas have already sawn the boards. If, in the meantime, some wealthy American will be good enough to get me some windows, we shall have a beautiful little chapel."

The next year found him at work once again. "The new church had to be built about ten miles from the sea on the top of a hill so steep that three yoke of oxen had all they could do to drag our empty wagon to the summit. Besides, there was not even the semblance of a road. We had to leap from one rock to another up the slope under the rays of an unbearable sun.

"I hit upon the plan of having all our Catholics go down to the beach with the coming of evening. Men, women and children slept out in the open that night, using stones as pillows. As dawn broke, after prayers in common, we all took to the path leading up the mountainside, each carrying a load accommodated to his strength, some with planks, some with joists, etc. Brother Calixte came to raise the framework, which goes up just as quickly as we hand him the wood – to the satisfaction of everyone concerned. The church is now finished and the bishop will bless it in the month of May. Please God, I will begin another one next year about thirty miles from here."

However, they did not wait until May to celebrate the successful accomplishment of the project, and at Epiphany they arranged a banquet as great their fatigue had been in the building of the chapel.

"On the eve of the celebration everyone was on hand and everything was ready. All went to the new church, which was too small, alas, for the throng that had gathered. I gave a sermon in which, after appropriate congratulations and exhortations, I urged my people to welcome their co-religionists who had come from afar to share their festival. For the people living in the locality had been called upon to furnish the food: the men, the beef; the women and children, the pork. Nearly a thousand persons partook of the banquet spread out on the grass all around the church. There were neither tables nor chairs, but each one sat tailor-fashion on the ground to eat. Besides, there were neither spoons nor forks, for out here even the most fastidious eat with their fingers. As for me, I spent the afternoon in the confessional. The next day, we had a sung Mass."

This banquet did not minimize by a hair the splendor of the feast which some months later marked the coming of Bishop Maigret:

"I went to meet him on my mule. Then we rode back together about a hundred miles and crossed one hundred and twenty streams. On Sunday, we stopped near a chapel I had built the year before. We came next to the mountain where, as I have related before, I once lost my way.

"When we arrived at our destination, the bishop, who had urgent business awaiting him at home, wished to proceed at once with the consecration. But my people had other plans. They asked for ten days in which to send invitations to the Catholics of the surrounding districts and to prepare a fitting festival. The bishop saw the wisdom of yielding; and he was rewarded with scenes of indescribable enthusiasm. My catechist had called upon each resident Catholic to furnish a pig. A whole herd of them was slaughtered, not to mention the oxen required for the menu. The banqueters ate until nothing remained but the bones. Then the bishop proceeded to the ceremony of the blessing of the church."

We have just been introduced to a catechist busy gathering pigs: he was one of the many co-workers and deputies Father Damien had trained. The missioner could not be everywhere at once. Thus, he kept his eye open for suitable assistants.

When he had discovered some promising young man, he gave particular care to his instruction, expounding to him the readings of the Mass so that he might be able to preach, and explaining religious truths more thoroughly to him so that he might be able to teach others. When the process was finished, he appointed him as a catechist or "prayer leader." On Sundays when Father was present, the prayer leader's role was minor. But Father was at hand only rarely, and in the intervals between his appearances it was the duty of the catechist to take care of the flock. He summoned the faithful to the church, took charge of the congregation, led in the singing of hymns and explained the word of God; he also prepared catechumens for baptism and, in general, kept the community alive until the pastor could visit it again.

Some catechists were remarkably successful: "I have managed to form some of them into preachers of eloquence and sound doctrine. Quite often they attract larger congregations than I do. Unbelievers prefer their preaching to mine; they take pleasure in listening to them, but are only bored when I say Mass, the meaning of which they do not understand at all."

Damien deplored the sophistication of young Kanakas. "They are scarcely able to talk when they are found to be familiar with what young theology students have yet to learn in theory. Parents utter all manner of indecencies in their hearing and initiate them into the most abominable practices. The dissolute habits of our natives bring upon them diseases which age them prematurely and make them easy victims of any contagion, to which they quickly succumb."

These children were rather slow in absorbing religious instruction: "They take easily to reading and ciphering, but they are reluctant to study the catechism. It is only by dint of repeating the same thing a hundred times that we can teach them even what is absolutely necessary."

The Work Progresses

When Damien arrived at Kohala, schooling was completely in the hands of non-Catholics, with consequent danger to the faith of young Catholics. In 1865, the government began to follow a policy of neutrality in school matters. Damien profited from this innovation by reviving old schools and establishing new ones; by sheer insistence, he secured teachers of his own choice, for whom the state contributed an allotment of sixty-five cents a day. The authorities even offered to underwrite his sending to the sisters at Honolulu certain native girls who, having been trained, were to return to conduct schools in his district. Thus, with the number of Catholic schools steadily increasing, the way was opened for a better future for his young people.

Despite the favorable developments, the apostle could not resist groaning under his burden of excessive work and, like the wood-cutter in the fable, looking forward to death for relief: "Generally speaking, I have few consolations to counterbalance my many vexations. Without divine grace, it would hardly be possible to consider as sweet and light the grievous load that rests upon my shoulders. Thus, at times I am reduced to the point of finding some pleasure in the thought that my end is coming nearer all the time."

It is a question whether such fits of depression lasted longer than it takes to describe them. Nevertheless, on certain days his loneliness of spirit plagued him and brought on what he called "black thoughts." When in his younger days the sights on a Paris street had troubled his innocent soul, at least he had been able to get away from them. But how could he avoid contact with this Hawaiian corruption? It gave rise, he said, "to a melancholy at times unbearable." Despite this, his conscience was good, his interior life was sound, the work of God which he was accomplishing consoled him, his superiors understood him, his Kanakas took kindly to him, the blows of human malice had not yet fallen on him and he had not lost his pleasant disposition.

The father general, however, would have to be made aware that he needed a companion: first, because the soul of a priest cannot find satisfaction in unrelieved association with licentious natives; secondly, because a priest must have the opportunity of regular confession in accordance with the practice of good Catholics and the prescription of the Picpus Rule. "Every two or three months, I try to go to see Father Charles at Hilo or Father Regis at Kona," he wrote. "That is not enough! But how can I do better, when each confession means one hundred fifty miles or more of travel?"

There was still another reason the father general must be informed: "If I complain of being alone, it is because I am thinking of the children of whom I am the father in Jesus Christ and who, in the absence of the priest, die without the sacraments despite all the efforts I make."

Without let-up, he asked his superiors for an assistant. At first, they turned a deaf ear. Was there no one among the younger religious who felt drawn to Hawaii? At any rate, there was Pamphile at Louvain, who at one time had longed for the missions and by this late date must surely have fully recovered from his typhus. For many a long year, Damien urged Pamphile to come to join him.

In 1866, he prevailed upon his provincial to write to the father general: "Good Father Damien has requested me to ask you for his brother for our mission. In his opinion, he (Pamphile) would adjust himself very well here. I leave it to your good judgment." But the good judgment of the superiors kept Pamphile at his teaching.

The missionary at Kohala was piqued by the decision. "Should I congratulate you?!" he wrote to the one concerned. "Here you are in the road to honors instead of being a poor missionary among savages.... How inscrutable are the designs of Providence!"

Time passed. Providence sent Pamphile to Louvain University to take his degrees in theology. Damien understood less and less the reasons for this turn of affairs. "And as for you, my dear brother," he wrote in 1870, "must I give up hope of ever seeing you here? Why do you aim at winning a doctor's hat at the cost of the salvation of some wretched Kanakas? Remember that you became a religious in order to be a missionary and that it was you who once criticized my lack of enthusiasm for the missions. I was very sorry to learn that in 1867 you rejected the appeal of the Very Reverend Father General and that another man had to go in your place, as I had done in 1863."

Pamphile did not deserve such censures, despite the decided views of Damien, who had not been taken into the confidence of his superiors. Damien's letter ended on a more pleasant note. It boasted of the delights of the Hawaiian cookery, which Pamphile would be able to sample if he would but consent to come: "I shall give you some excellent coffee, which I make very strong. While I have neither milk nor butter, I do have honey and eggs. I also have an oven in which I can bake very fine bread. I have so much ham that you will never be without it. I have just bought two horses: they will also be at your disposal. Don't delay, then, lazybones!"

But Pamphile did not come. Later, in 1895, well after Damien had quit this world, he tried to carry out his brother's wishes and came to take his place among the lepers. A book man, a theologian, a Hebrew scholar, a philologist, placid and absent-minded, Pamphile was not at all made for the life of a missionary. He stayed only twenty months on Molokai, after which he returned to Europe to teach sacred sciences to his confreres.

At last, Father Gulstan Ropert landed at Kohala. On January 11, 1869, Damien wrote: "Father Gulstan, as well as Brothers Boniface and Quentin are reported on the way. But when will they arrive? Shall I get only one of them when I need a dozen?" In April, he concluded his letter, which had been interrupted in the writing three months back: "Today I am no longer alone. Father Gulstan has come to be my assistant."

Father Damien and Father Ropert worked together in complete harmony and perfect charity. "Together we built many chapels and lived like two brothers," wrote Ropert later, after he had become a bishop. "We built...."

The following letter, which is dated 1872, recalls these constructions made in common. It is to be noted that Damien says "I" where the bishop says "We." It will also be noted that Damien still deplores the academic vocation of his brother. His irony will appear perhaps a little heavy-handed and trenchant, but it should be borne in mind that he did not have a competent grasp of the nuances of the French words he employed:

"You seem to be much put out with me, my dear brother, since for the past three years you have not bothered to write me. Is it possible you regarded as insults the mild reproofs I addressed to you in October, 1870? Pardon me, I beg you, for those little sins of rudeness...."

He passed on to the Franco-Prussian War, which for him was still a topic of current interest.

"Then, are you still a teacher at Versailles? The newspapers informed us that that town was occupied by the Prussians. They also called attention to the loyalty of many priests who distinguished themselves on that occasion, but they made no mention of you. Would you have been faint-hearted enough to fear cannonballs? I should never have believed that of a Belgian from Tremeloo."

There followed the description of a missionary's Sunday: "Once the hard work of the morning is finished, the dinner horn blows. We eat what Providence sends. A gourd of *poi*, always full, serves as the main dish. Meat is not lacking, nor water, of course. Coffee and bread are sometimes available; beer or wine, never. The plates are not always washed. As I have to work all week long, my hands are not so clean as yours, which are employed only to turn the pages of a book. But habit and hunger make one eat just the same. For dessert, I smoke a pipe.

"When this is over, no time is lost in getting on horseback. I must hasten to another Catholic settlement. If I must celebrate a second Mass, as is often the case, my breakfast is postponed until two or three o'clock. And I end the day either in the confessional or in teaching theology to the catechists, my deputies. When evening comes, I am completely done in. But the more tired I am, the happier I feel."

That was a Sunday. As for the weekdays: "First, my Mass; then, often, instructions; then breakfast; always *poi*! For at least seven months I have eaten no other food. Then I take off my cassock, I pick up a saw, and I work as a carpenter; for it is only at the cost of much sweat that I have succeeded in having fairly decent churches everywhere. I have also built some in the district of good little Father Gulstan. A hurricane razed his house and two of his chapels. What trouble I have had in rebuilding them!"

The destructive hurricane just referred to by Damien had actually been less terrible than the earthquake of fifteen months earlier.

There had been advance signs of its coming all through the month of March, when ground quavers, at first light and intermittent, then stronger and more frequent, gave notice of the explosion of subterranean forces. Toward the end of the month, as many as three hundred violent tremors could be counted in a twenty-four hour period.

On April 2, the cataclysm broke in its full horror on the south end of the island. The ground heaved, sank back again and cracked open. Bells in the churches rang violently without a hand at the rope. The forest reeled and trees were uprooted, falling one across the other, the noise of their crashing mingled with the shrieks of the wind. The verses of the psalm were verified to the letter: "The mountains skipped like rams, the hills like lambs." Rocky avalanches roared down into the valleys. The side of a mountain was blasted loose and thrown far and wide across the floor of the valley below it, while its stones and debris, falling like meteorites, destroyed people, animals and houses. At Kau, the earth burst asunder, making an opening through which poured a gigantic river of stones and mud 10,000 yards wide. In its first gushing, it spread to a point five miles distant, flowing over everything in its way and bringing with its scalding flood instant death to herds of steers and flocks of goats along with thirty-one herdsmen.

The disaster was even more frightful at Apoua, where the whole island seemed destined to be swallowed by the waters. Convulsed by some sub-marine volcanoes, the sea at first receded as if to get headway for a leap, then began to move forward again, with its boiling surface now higher by thirty feet than at the fullest tide; and gathering speed as it rushed forward with terrifying roar, it obliterated everything in its path. Men, women and children, boats and houses all disappeared in a maelstrom of trees, planks, animals and debris torn from the cliffs. After several such assaults by the sea, not a trace was left of the fishing villages that had once lined this shore.

On April 7, the last act of this drama was played. The volcano chose that day to vomit from its many mouths enormous rocks and streams of molten stone which ran in rivers of lava to overtake and destroy a great number of doomed people who were vainly trying to flee.

Damien was fortunate enough to escape death. But almost all his churches and schools had collapsed and many of his neophytes had perished. He was not the man, however, to wring his hands in vain sorrow over his losses. Loaded down with food and clothing, he set out in search of survivors, and later he turned to rebuilding his ruined chapels with the same ardor with which he had first raised them.

"I am neither a poet nor a good writer," he confessed once. He took up the pen only in case of necessity; when, for example, he had to buy some lumber at Honolulu, or give to his superiors a report on the state of his mission, or to send a bit of news about himself to Tremeloo.

On June 8, 1869, he wrote to Father Modeste, asking him to ship a "thousand shingles"; on the 21st of the same month, he begged his pardon for going into debt to purchase an urgently needed wagon; on December 27, he sent his New Year wishes: "Your pardon for everything I have done in the past year which might have displeased you. Come what will, I wish sincerely that we may be able always to live in harmony." Thereupon, in accordance with the Rule, he lay before his superior the spiritual and temporal conditions of his parish. He reported 39 baptisms – 25 administered to adults, 14 to children – and seven marriages blessed. There were 40 chickens, three horses and one mule in his possession at that time. He would have had more if he had not contributed two horses and a mule to outfit Father Gulstan, who had recently landed and another mule to Father Charles who, as everyone knew, had let his own mule die of hunger. He then listed the expenditures of the year:

2 chickens and 1 pig	$1.00
2 bags of salt	1.00
1 saddle and 1 bridle	7.00
2 horses	10.00

He also listed a pair of boots, which cost as much as a horse, and finally a host of purchases necessitated by the buildings then in the process of construction.

By way of summary, he had received $279.00 and had spent $271.00. His bank balance was $8.00.

On December 26, 1870, Damien reported for the year 29 baptisms and eight marriages. He owned four horses and one mule, four cows, for which he had paid $17.00, "many chickens," which he did not bother to count, and "some sheep," of which he did not give the exact number. His bank balance had improved to the extent of a surplus of $62.00. Some of his income had come to him by way of inheritance: "Ten months ago, an old man asked me to let him have a place in my house so that I might take care of him for what remained of his life and see to his burial after his death. He has left me his entire fortune: $100.00, two horses and a cast-iron frying pan."

He remained strongly attached to his relatives and, at that time, wrote to them once a year.

He was to always make it a point to avoid alarming his aged parents, and even after he had become a leper, he would continue to say that things were not too bad.

Little accustomed to writing, his father and mother depended on Pamphile to carry on what correspondence was necessary. Pamphile, on his part, was absorbed in his studies and his teaching.

When after a delay of nine months a reply to a letter of his arrived from Tremeloo, Damien rejoiced: "I have received your letter with a joy I cannot express. You are right, dear father, to be concerned a little less about your temporal affairs in order to give more thought to eternity! It is thinking about eternity which has led half of your children to the cloister and has driven me to ever greater devotion to duty."

In 1872, he was worried: "What has happened to you, my dear Parents? It is three years since I have had any word from you. Are you both still alive? Perhaps the Lord has.... In that case, his will be done! But, at least, relieve me of my uncertainty. As for me, thank God I'm still strong and in good health, and I am always happy."

Then he spoke to them of the churches he had built and of Janneke Roof, the carpenter of Tremeloo, to whom he could now give a few pointers; of the War of 1870; of each member of the family; of the progress of the Faith in his distant islands, which he was destined never to leave: "It is only in heaven," he said, "that we shall see one another again."

At another time, he sent a letter to his brothers: "Our mother writes me that you each have three children. Leonce's son, John, must be big by this time. Let him study well now, and when he is fourteen, he will start Latin. Tell him that I am waiting for him out here, that I already have two saddle-horses for him. As for you, my dear brothers, remember that, of us eight children, you alone are in a position to assist our dear parents in their old age. I humbly ask you to act as my substitute in rendering them the filial affection and care they could have looked for from me. Show them the greatest respect and never say a word to hurt them. Live in peace; cherish your children and bring them up in the fear of God. I am looking forward to a letter from you. Your devoted brother, Joseph."

His sister Pauline was a religious in Holland. There had been no sign of life from her in a long time. Was she ill? Might she be dead? "Three years have passed, my dear sister, since you sent me a line.... Write to me, I beg you. Have a little regard for your poor missionary brother who, if he is left forgotten among savages, will soon become a savage himself. But, the thought occurs to me, could the reason for your silence be that you are off for heaven already? I hope not." As a matter of fact, less than a year later Pauline did die in her convent in Uden.

Like those untroubled souls that have realized the beautiful dreams of their childhood, he dwelt in the happy memories of the past: "I picked up your letter," he wrote to Pamphile, "in a port through which I passed in going to a place about sixty miles from here. All that night as I was making my way across the lava deposited recently by the volcano, I chewed upon the news you gave me. At one time, I was standing in the mill at Betecom with our brothers, Leonce and Gerard; at another time, at the death-bed of cousin Winck to whom, I trust, God will show mercy; again, with Pauline in her convent where reign the peace and happiness so foreign to the turbulent life of a missionary. I also accompanied you on your charming visit to Flanders. Where are the happy days, dear brother, when we lived together under the roof of our good parents, when we went off together to school at Werchter and later to the University of Louvain? The beautiful hours of childhood are gone beyond recall! Now middle age has arrived when we keep on courageously ploughing the field of the Lord, you in Europe (perhaps?), I in the Sandwich Islands. But if you cannot come in person to join me here, at least train, from among your pupils, some sturdy and virtuous men, fearless and strong in charity, to come to take our places when we shall have entered into eternal rest."

On July 14, 1872, Damien wrote again to Pamphile:

"Now I have need of nothing more: I have beautiful chapels, decent priest-houses, chickens and pigs in abundance and wide fields to furnish their food and my own. This year I shall be freer to devote myself to the care of the sick and the dying, at least until Providence sees fit to send me to other worries."

Was this a presentiment? In point of fact, the year would not end before Damien would leave Kohala for Molokai to work out his final destiny.

Part Two

Among the Lepers

Chapter 7

Molokai

The Island of Molokai lies at the center of the Hawaiian Archipelago, with Oahu to the northwest and Maui to the southeast. It extends east to west and is shaped somewhat like a willow leaf or a fish lying on its side. The Kanakas call it the "land of precipices," so steep and difficult a terrain have the volcanoes fashioned for it. Its face is desolate, in contrast with the smiling beauty of the neighboring islands. In 1873, not more than 2,000 people tried to make a home on it.

From the north shore of Molokai, the promontory of Kalawao pushes out into the sea. It is a tongue of land, about ten square miles in extent, with high cliffs called "Pali" rising about fifteen hundred feet above the peninsula at its juncture with the island proper. At the center of this promontory yawns a crater about 65 yards wide and 30 feet deep. A sterile plain falls away from the crater in every direction; it is strewn with great rocks, occasional clumps of tall, smooth grass, thickets of old pandanus trees and long-leaved reeds. Bounded on three sides by cliffs that drop abruptly to the sea and hemmed in on the fourth, or southern, border by the almost insurmountable barrier of the "Pali," this place seems to have been made for enclosing banished convicts and preventing their escape.

Instead, this was the spot chosen by the Hawaiian authorities for the segregation of the archipelago's lepers. It was here that Father Damien would spend the last sixteen years of his life.

Leprosy

Until recent times, leprosy, or Hansen's disease, has been regarded as the most horrible of all diseases.

It is as old as the human race, appearing sometimes here, sometimes there, then vanishing for no known reason, but never ceasing to ravage some section of the globe.

The existence of Hansen's disease 6,000 years ago is attested in a papyrus preserved in Berlin,. Other documents refer to its presence in China in 2,000 B.C. and in Japan in 1,500 B.C. The Levitical laws are evidence that in the days of Moses leprosy was quite common among the Jews who, probably infected by the Egyptians, doubtlessly passed the disease on to the Syrians and others.

There are some records of Hansen's disease in Europe from the fourth century on. The twelfth and thirteenth centuries, especially, saw it overrun the continent. Toward 1150 it had taken root in England, Scotland, France, Spain, the Low Countries, Scandinavia and Russia. In the twelfth century, London had seven lazarettos or leper-hospitals. (The word lazaretto comes from Lazarus, the leper of the Gospels whose sores the dogs licked at the gates of the wicked rich man.) Soon every French town had its leprosarium. Various religious orders were established to care for lepers.

Since leprosy was known to be contagious, its victims were isolated as a measure of protection.

Under the title: *The Manner of Putting Lepers Outside the Community*, old rituals set down the steps in the ceremony called *separatio leprosorum*.

The suspect was cited before an ecclesiastical judge, and, once he was declared a leper, he was obliged to cut himself off from the human community. First, he attended Mass, on his knees before the altar with a black veil over his face. Then, the officiating priest let fall on his head three shovelfuls of earth while saying: "*Sis mortuus mundo, vivus iterum Deo*—Be dead to the world, living henceforth to God." In some dioceses, this rite was performed in the cemetery, where the diseased person descended into a symbolic grave. Then a copy was given to him of the following "Prohibitions" after they had been read aloud to him before witnesses:

"I forbid you ever to enter a church, market, mill or public bakehouse and all groups and assemblies of people.

"I forbid you even to wash your hands or any other thing required by you in fountains or brooks; if you wish to drink, you are to take up the water with your jug or some other vessel.

"I forbid you henceforth to go without your leper garb in which you will be recognized by others, or to walk unshod or barefoot except within your own house.

"I forbid you to touch anything you wish to buy except with a staff or a rod to indicate what you are selecting.

"I forbid you henceforth to enter taverns or other houses if you wish to buy wine or to take and receive offerings; see to it that these are put into your jug or some other vessel.

"I forbid you to be in the company of any woman but your own.

"I forbid you, in traveling through the countryside, to answer anyone who addresses you without first going to the side of the road away from the wind, for fear that you infect someone; and, also, in the future to go along a narrow path for fear that you meet someone on it.

"I forbid you, unless necessity requires it, to travel by minor roads or over meadows, or to touch hedges and bushes before putting on your gloves.

"I forbid you to touch children or young people whoever they may be, or to give anything to them or to anyone else.

"I forbid you henceforth to eat or drink in the company of others, except lepers."

The priest added:

"However, you will not take offense at being segregated from other people, inasmuch as such separation pertains only to the body; as for the spirit, which is paramount, you are always with us and will share in all the prayers of Our Holy Mother Church, just as if you were daily assisting in person with the others at divine services."

The outcast was then led in a procession to his hut in the middle of a field. Upon arriving there the leper said, "This retreat is mine. I will inhabit it permanently because I wish it that way." The priest forbade anyone to do him the slightest injury; then he urged the leper's parents to remain with him for another thirty-two hours to keep him from falling into despair. Thereupon, after blessing the following objects, the priest held them out to the hermit: the black cloak he would have to wear, the clappers with which he would signal his approach, the gloves, the small jug, the wallet and some other serviceable articles.

After the fourteenth century, Hansen's disease rapidly declined in Europe, but toward the middle of the sixteenth century it was found among the emigrants to America.

Aretaeus, a physician who lived in Rome in the reign of Nero, gave this description of leprosy:

"It appears on the face, the ears and the extremities in the shape of shiny tubercles of various sizes, some of deep red, some of an ashen grey color; the skin thickens and becomes rough and partially or completely dead to feeling; the hair falls out everywhere except from the scalp; the sides of the nose swell, the nostrils expand; the lips become bloated; the outer ear, particularly the lobe, stretches, thickens and breaks out with tubercles; the skin of the cheeks and the forehead coarsens, inflates and forms large bulging wrinkles especially over the eyes.... The voice becomes hoarse and muffled; the sensitivity of the affected parts diminishes or disappears completely; the subject can be pinched or cut without his feeling anything.... At a more advanced stage of the affliction, the tumors break open and finally ulcerate. Ulcerations appear in the throat and in the nose, destroying the palate and the nasal partitions; the nose sags in; the breath becomes unbearable; gangrene attacks the fingers and the toes, destroying the ligaments."

It was not until 1873 that the Norwegian, Dr. Hansen, discovered the bacillus of leprosy, and not until 1881 that Neisser of Breslau found the means of isolating and studying it. "This bacillus, similar to that of tuberculosis, is disseminated in the tissues, especially inside the leprous cells, which it distends like pincushions.... The method of transmission of the disease is not known; but it is understood that it does not attack animals and that a healthy person will not fall victim except through prolonged contact with some leper."

The Hell of Kalawao

It is probable that Hansen's disease appeared in Hawaii long before people recognized it as such. In 1823, Reverend Steward, a Protestant missionary, wrote: "Cases of ophthalmic scrofula and of elephantiasis are very common here." Was this the horrible scourge?

In 1850, the government at Honolulu set up a Board of Health charged with "taking measures to protect the people and to cure them of epidemic diseases, in particular cholera." There was no mention of leprosy, of which only a single case had been verified.

In 1863, a member of the Board of Health, Doctor Hillebrand, raised his voice to direct attention to the fact that in the country many lepers were spreading the infection. His colleagues delayed eight months before appointing a doctor to inquire into the matter.

In the meantime, foreigners had taken alarm and conducted a vigorous newspaper campaign. On January 3, 1865, before the investigation was completed, King Kamehameha V issued a decree aimed at calming their fears.

The decree obliged lepers to make themselves known and the Board of Health to take a census of suspects. The incurables were to be sent to the "leprosarium" of Molokai; and the other victims were to be cared for at the Hospital of Kahili near Honolulu.

These measures were highly unpopular. The newspapers had insisted in vain that Kahili had every remedy required to cure the less seriously affected and that Molokai was fitted out to allow the incurables to end their days in comfort. The lepers would have none of it. Sooner than go far from home to die abandoned, they preferred to suffer on and wait for death in their own poor huts surrounded by their families. Parents refused to permit their children to go; husbands and wives declined to separate; old people were unwilling to leave the place where they had spent their lives.

Force had to be called into play. Doctors summoned the police to accompany them. Beaters, as in a hunt, took up positions over the countryside and tracked down the sick people like so many game animals. With the connivance of friends, these unfortunates sought out inaccessible retreats, took refuge in the depths of the ravines or went underground in caves from which they emerged only at night. They fled at the approach of any human being.

For the first eight months, this man-hunt yielded no bag to speak of. Both the sick and the whole stood at bay against the agents of the Board. On the Island of Kauai, a Doctor Smith and many of his assistants were massacred. In other places, police agents were mortally wounded. For a long time, investigators on the Island of Oahu were welcomed with shots from Winchester rifles.

However, some cripples who were unable to flee were captured. In the long run, force was successful; before the end of 1866, one hundred forty-one lepers were driven on board ship at Honolulu.

The departure was attended by distressing scenes. "What a sight!" said one witness. "The sick person was accompanied by his parents, who hugged him, covered him with countless kisses and mingled their tears with his. When the sick were finally torn away and put on the steamer, soul-shaking cries of despair and howls of grief rose to rend the air."

These wretched people were transported to the shores of Molokai, where there were at that time two "villages": Kalaupapa and Kalawao, separated by about three miles and boasting in all fourteen huts and about forty natives. The landing-place was at Kalaupapa. The lepers were rowed ashore here and later taken to Kalawao.

Contrary to the newspaper reports, there was nothing prepared for their reception save a nondescript hospital, reserved for the worst cases, lacking both beds and doctors. Such victims as were received there entered only to die, lying on the floor or on straw mats spread on the ground. As for the others, they crowded into huts that had been abandoned by their native owners, departing for the near-by valleys.

The Board of Health fondly believed that, once the lepers were installed on the island, the more able-bodied among them would set cheerfully to work at cultivating the soil, thus providing for the needs of all. It would suffice, thought the Board, to send an occasional shipment of meat and clothing to meet any extra needs.

The event belied the hopes of the Board. No one went to work. There were no medicines. Shipments of food were irregular and inadequate. From 1866 to 1873, almost forty percent of these exiles died; exactly 311 out of 797.

It is impossible to describe in full detail what happened there.

Ambrose Hutchinson, a leper who lived at the lazaretto for half a century, gave this account:

"On the day after my arrival, I saw a man with a bandaged face leave his house pushing a wheelbarrow filled with rags. Out of curiosity, I followed him. When he arrived at the place called *Hoopau Keaho*, "the place of death," he tipped his load into the ravine, then quietly went back to his house. I had heard a cry. I went to investigate and discovered an unfortunate soul in his death agony. It was he who had cried out when he hit the bottom of the ditch. In my indignation, I denounced the affair to my new companions, who showed no surprise because I was telling them nothing new."

Except for a few who had money, those who died in Molokai had benefit of neither coffin nor burial service. When a fellow-leper was good enough to wait for a sick person to die before getting rid of him, he rolled up the corpse in a blanket which was fastened by means of ropes tied at the neck, back and ankles; then he passed a pole through this bundle. The corpse, thus trussed up and swung beneath the pole, was carried by two men to its last resting place. It was buried in a grave so shallow that hogs came later to eat the carcass.

From despair, these unfortunates sank into bestiality.

No one made any attempt to alleviate their suffering or to retard its progress. The doctor rarely put in an appearance. The lepers had been bereft of parents, home and affection. No one cared even about checking their rising resentment. Neither work nor diversion was furnished to take their minds off their misery. No priest was at hand to speak to them about their souls or to pray with them.

No longer supported by any reason for living, they gave up

all sense of dignity and all desire for cleanliness and order. They had been treated like mangy animals that are driven away from sight; and being no longer respected as human beings, they proceeded to make beasts of themselves.

"*Aole kanawai me keia wahi.* This place has no law." Such was the greeting with which old-timers met new arrivals. It was a maxim all observed. In the uninhibited idleness, time was spent in sleeping, playing cards, drinking and indulging in vice. Here was a branch-office of Sodom.

What did the authorities at Honolulu do in the face of such anarchy? Almost nothing.

Did they lack heart? Did they close their eyes in order not to see? Beset by the difficulties of a land on the way to losing its independence, did they find themselves distracted by politics? It is not our purpose to answer such questions. But affairs were conducted as if the whole administrative problem had been solved by withdrawing lepers from circulation.

The Board of Health sent to the leprosarium a superintendent, who in turn drew assistants in happy-go-lucky fashion from among the sick and various undesirables.

The first superintendent was a Frenchman named Lepart. He confined himself to sending the Board reports about the revolts and orgies, in the face of which he felt powerless; and about the absence of shelter, clothing and food, which made the colony resentful. He came away without having remedied anything.

His successor was Mr. Walsh, a Briton, who brought along his wife under the title of "nurse of the lazaretto." Largely through the assistance of a group of police, composed of some healthy men who had joined their leprous wives, he succeeded in establishing a degree of order. It was unfortunate that neither he nor his helpmate understood Hawaiian. Mr. Walsh built a cottage for himself, erected a school for children, improved the hospital fare and imported some cows. He undoubtedly would have effected still other improvements if he had not died prematurely.

For some time, Mrs. Walsh carried on in her husband's place. Then, an old retired sailor was given to her as an assistant, but he did not get along well with her. Soon mutinies were breaking out, worse than before. Then the leper Koholuli, a former captain with a will of iron, was appointed director. He severely punished the two ring leaders, put down the rebellion for the time being, and then dropped from view without achieving any other results.

Affairs ran along in this fashion until in 1873 King Lunalilo mounted the throne.

However, the public was beginning to get some of the facts and was becoming indignant. A wave of pity soon spread over the whole archipelago and the voices of some men of spirit were raised through the press.

One of these latter, publicly petitioned the king to go to the spot and see for himself how the lepers were being treated. Lunalilo contented himself with drawing up a message of sympathy, which was published in *The Hawaiian Gazette* of May 14. To this platonic manifesto, the newspaper added the observation: "Those whom the lepers most need are a priest and a doctor who would sacrifice themselves for the lepers by imprisoning themselves with them."

The next day, Walter Gibson wrote in the *Nuhou*: "He would be a noble soul, forever deserving the blessing of humanity, who would consent to go to the assistance of these poor people! Is there, then, a priest who will be inspired to turn his steps toward them and to offer the sacrifice of his life?"

One month later that appeal was heard and that wish magnificently gratified.

Chapter 8

"This is for Life"

On May 4, 1873, Bishop Maigret consecrated a new church at Wailuku on the Island of Maui. Six Picpus fathers from the neighboring districts assisted at the ceremony. Father Damien hastened to go from Kohala to join his confreres at Wailuku and to spend several days in their company.

The conversation of these missionaries turned to the lepers isolated at Kalawao, whose destitution had stirred the whole Archipelago. Naturally, the condition of the Catholics among these wretches worried them.

Up to this time, the Mission had been obliged to neglect Molokai to some extent. Once a year, a Father would go there for a stay of two or three days.

In 1871, Father Raymond remained there for several weeks and went about among the lepers. They manifested such joy and showed such good dispositions that the bishop resolved to build a chapel for them. Brother Bertrand erected it in six weeks. On May 30, 1872, it was ready for the return of Father Raymond, who solemnized the day by administering baptism to twelve candidates.

In the lenten season of 1873, Father Boniface visited the

lepers. Ninety of them made their Easter Duty; and a former prayer-leader from the Island of Oahu died so edifying a death that Father mentioned it in a letter to his provincial:

"In spite of unspeakable sufferings, the dying man remained fully resigned. He pressed to his heart the crucifix, his rosary and his prayerbook—his most precious possessions in this world, said he. When I was giving him Holy Viaticum, he held his prayerbook in his two remaining fingers in order to read from it the prayers before and after Communion. He begged me to stay at his side till he drew his last breath. His agony was not over until the next day. Three old men were so impressed that they asked for baptism as soon as possible."

This anecdote and others like it were told by some of the missionaries in the group as Damien listened. The lepers, it was recalled, gathered each Sunday at their chapel to pray, to sing, to recite the rosary; they had asked for the stations of the cross, so that in the midst of their own sufferings they might be consoled by contemplating the sufferings of the Savior.

At length, the bishop, who was listening to this conversation, mentioned a petition the lepers had recently addressed to him asking for a resident priest.

Even in the preceding year, when Brother Bertrand had been busy in his workyard, the lepers had approached to ask him to transmit their grievances: "Speak for us to *Lui Ka Epikopo*, to Louis, our bishop. Tell him that it is not enough for us to see a priest once a year. There is so much time to die between visits! And without a priest, how shall we save our souls?"

The bishop told his group of missionaries that he had decided to grant the request for a resident priest. No people in the Archipelago had greater need of a pastor than these outcasts. But whom should he appoint to administer that perilous post? Was he not sentencing to death the man he would send there? A superior is loath to issue an order under such circumstances. Bishop Maigret expressed his wishes in general terms. A system of rotation could be arranged, he said, with some of the younger missionaries taking turns at the lazaretto. To begin with....

At this point Damien leaped to his feet to break in before the others could say a word.

"I—I want to go there!" he said. "I know many of these unfortunate souls, and I ask only to share their lot and their prison."

"I should not even have wished to lay this burden on you, but since you are volunteering, I accept your offer gladly," replied the old bishop, as he pressed the head of his great-hearted son to his breast.

In a letter written three months later, Father Damien had mentioned that some presentiments had paved the way for his decision:

"When the agents of the Board (of Health) came to carry off some of my faithful, a voice within me told me that I should rejoin them some day. When I took the ship to Wailuku, the same voice warned me that I should never return to Kohala, that I should never again see my well-beloved children nor the beautiful chapels I had built. For this reason, there were tears in my eyes when I turned away from that Catholic settlement to which I had become attached during the eight years I had spent in it."

Arrival

On May 10, the *Kilauea* put out from the Island of Maui with a draft of fifty lepers and a cargo of some cattle for the lazaretto. The bishop and Damien were on its deck, as toward noon it approached Kalaupapa. When the resident lepers caught sight of them, "those who were able to walk ran down from Kalawao," related the bishop. "Our neophytes surrounded us, their rosaries hanging from their necks.... How great was their joy, when I presented to them the man who had asked to come to them and was henceforth to be their father! They cast themselves on their knees with tears brimming in their eyes."

Theoretically, Father Damien had come for just a few weeks. Others were to relieve him. But as soon as the bishop had returned to the boat, the priest began to write letter after letter to his superiors.

On May 12, he begged his provincial to have Father Gulstan, his neighbor on the Island of Hawaii, watch over Kohala, his former district: "until I return, unless you should find someone to take my place there for good, for I am bent on devoting my life to the lepers. It is absolutely necessary for a priest to live here. The afflicted are coming here by the boat-load." He had left Kohala bringing with him nothing but his breviary. "Send me some wine and some altar breads, some books of spiritual reading, some rosaries, some shirts, trousers, shoes, a bag of flour and a bell."

At the end of forty-eight hours, he was laying plans for settling down:

"While waiting for you to send me some lumber to build a house, I am living under a pandanus tree."

Eight days later, he was working without let-up: "There is something to occupy my time from morning to night. I have on my lists two hundred and ten Catholic lepers and twenty catechumens.... Tell me whether you and the bishop have decided upon the fortunate priest selected to remain here."

The provincial replied: "A final decision has not yet been made. You can remain at Molokai, following your heart's desire until further orders."

There was no other time in his life when Damien had written so many letters. Without prejudice to obedience, he wanted his superiors to realize that it was his desire to stay on Molokai. On May 25, he told Father Modeste that he had come upon "a group of Catholics, in one of the valleys, who had not yet set an eye on a priest in ten years. Again, while administering the anointing of the sick to a schoolboy leper, I uncovered his foot, which was being eaten by worms." Was there not enough in such news to soften the heart of the old provincial?

On May 28, Damien apologized for his inability to take his ministry to the natives beyond the Pali. There were two hundred Catholics over there whom he would go to see later on; but visiting the sick now took him "four to five days from morning to evening."

If Damien had been in a position to read what on that same date the provincial at Honolulu was writing to the general at Paris, his mind would have been relieved. His case had been won. The Hawaiian press had forced the hand of his superiors.

Without a single dissenting voice, newspapers of all factions were praising "the heroism of the Belgian priest who has volunteered to live among the lepers." One of them described with some feeling the destitution of the Father, who had embraced the lepers' cause without making any previous preparations: "He is without shelter and has no more clothing than the sick people themselves." By now, gifts in abundance had begun to arrive for his relief. In less than a week, the Archipelago had come to know him as "the hero of Molokai." This title – which was to be his from that time forward – would never feed his pride, but would never cease to irritate some of his contemporaries.

Father Modeste did not find it prudent to put Damien on a pedestal at once. So far as he was concerned, all his religious were equal, or at least equally extraordinary. To his letter to the general, he added some excerpts from the newspapers and expressed his amazement that the press should raise such a hubbub about Damien, while they remained silent about Fathers Boniface and Raymond, who had only recently gone to visit the lepers, and about Brother Bertrand who had built a chapel for them. He put things in proper perspective by noting that many of his missionaries had volunteered for that post of honor. In spite of all this, he concluded, for fear of adverse public opinion they would have to recognize the advisability of leaving Damien where he was.

Settling Down

The presence of Father Damien brought new spirit to the lazaretto. A breath of hope blew over these hopeless folk. This handsome man in his early thirties—hearty and optimistic, laughing at trouble and feeling capable of dealing successfully with any difficulty—developed overnight into the sympathetic pastor of his sorry flock. Some people, even men of great virtue, have no affability to speak of. But the newcomer radiated love of his fellow men. He warmed all hearts and drew them to himself. The lepers knew that a friend had come among them. These big neglected children tasted the happiness of no longer being orphans.

"Joe, my boy, here you are for life!" said Damien to himself when the decision of his superiors reached him. More than once in the days to come, he would repeat these words, which forbade his looking back or dreaming of other things. So far as he was concerned, the bargain was sealed. He had entered the leprosarium as one enters the religious life, or as a man plights his troth to the woman he loves.

At the accession of Lunalilo on January 8, 1873, the members of the old, inefficient Board of Health were replaced. The new Board, and each succeeding Board, was composed of a president chosen from within the government, a secretary and some other prominent men. From its headquarters in Honolulu, the Board administered the leprosarium and made appointments to all its posts.

The chief of all the officials of the lazaretto was Superintendent Meyer, one of the principal landowners of Molokai, who remained in charge for thirty years. He lived with his large family at Kalae in the southern part of the island and only at long intervals did he go down among the lepers. He was assisted by an under-superintendent, who lived at the leprosarium and was in immediate command of the employees.

The new Board was not long in making its influence felt. It enlarged the hospital and installed some beds. It took special precaution against having any more lepers die of starvation. Every one of them was henceforth entitled to a monthly ration of five pounds of meat and twenty-one pounds of poi. Instead of meat, those who preferred it received twelve pounds of fish; and instead of poi, seven pounds of flour.

The lazaretto was a prison which never released its guests. Up to this time, however, the prisoners had been permitted to receive visitors. Some of these visitors had been slow in leaving. Wives who had rejoined their husbands, husbands who had rejoined their wives, parents who had come to their children — all had obtained permission to stay. Now this tolerant practice was ended; under the pretext of preventing contagion, access to the island was forbidden to all except lepers.

It should be observed that at that time some members of the Board were rather apprehensive and resentful: apprehensive, since out of fear of contracting leprosy, they never set foot on the island; resentful, because they did not relish the eulogies heaped by the press on the Catholic priest.

They criticized him for having gone to the island without official authorization. Public opinion would not tolerate their expelling him from the island; but they forbade him to leave the leprosarium "for fear," as their decree put it, "of propagating the disease abroad." They deceived themselves into thinking that, rather than submit to life imprisonment, Damien would leave of his own accord.

This decree did cause him bitter suffering. Certainly, the prospect of never again seeing his superior and his confreres was painful enough. But what depressed him more than all the other disabilities was the impossibility of going to confession in the future. Many religious make a rule of weekly confession. Damien was certainly not one of those who would be satisfied with confession once a month. He had a conscience that was very delicate, if not scrupulous. The episode about to be related makes it abundantly clear that his most cruel affliction at this time was the deprivation of a confessor.

He had been cut off from confession for more than four months when the *Kilauea* touched at Kalaupapa with its customary load of lepers and provisions. Knowing how much his son desired to see him, Father Modeste had taken passage on the little steamer. He wished to go ashore at Kalaupapa, but was prevented by the captain.

"I have formal orders," said the officer, "to keep you from landing."

After waiting for some time on the beach, Father Damien leaped into a skiff, rowed alongside the ship and prepared to climb aboard.

"Keep off! Keep off!" shouted the captain. "I have been strictly forbidden to allow you to communicate with anybody at all."

The poor priest then knelt in his skiff, raised tear-filled eyes to his provincial standing at the ship's rail and asked: "Is there anyone on board who understands French?"

"No," replied Father Modeste.

"Then, I beg you, hear my confession."

Damien thought that this would be his last opportunity to receive the Sacrament of Penance; hence, in a loud voice he made a general confession in French to Father Modeste. Leaning over the guard-rail, his elderly superior gave him absolution as the ship began to steam away.

Some weeks later, Father Aubert, also, made an attempt to bring some consolation to his ostracized confrere.

Disguised in civilian clothes, he landed on the southern shore of Molokai and set himself to scale the forbidding cliffs of the Pali: "Toward midnight," he wrote, "I reached the summit. The more difficult part lay ahead: the descent leading toward the lazaretto. For three hours, I let myself down the steep slopes, sliding on my back the greater part of the way."

He did not mention in what condition he finally arrived. After having heard Father Damien's confession, he returned to the island of Maui, confident that his disguise had been completely effective. The agents of the government, however, had been vigilant. "On my return, I had a visit from the police. I had been denounced to the government which, in turn, had complained to the bishop. The affair raised some commotion in Honolulu; but public opinion was on our side."

Not meeting with success in their efforts to expel Damien, his opponents proceeded to confine him within the limits of his own place. He had been forbidden to leave the island; now he was forbidden to travel about on it. He was prohibited from exercising his ministry as much among the lepers as among the natives who were living in the southern part of the island. Injustice was reduced to absurdity.

Later Damien told a visitor, Charles W. Stoddard, that once, on a visit to the southern district, he was invited to dinner by the island's chief of police. He accepted without suspicion and thus threw himself into the jaws of the wolf.

"Aren't you aware," said his host, "of the order I have received touching you?"

"No."

"Well, I am ordered to arrest you on sight!" concluded the police chief, laughing.

Toward the end of 1873, his opponents had to beat a retreat and leave Damien in peace for a while. The installation of a new administration in the government, as well as the humaneness of Superintendent Meyer, forced them to mitigate their hostility.

Damien was delighted to receive through the intervention

of the French consul, the following permission:

Honolulu, December 18, 1873

His Excellency, the President of the Board of Health, asks me to inform you of the receipt of your letter and he authorizes you to visit the leprosarium from time to time as circumstances demand. As evidence of this authorization, you can show these presents to the Superintendent of the asylum.

Your obedient servant

Gulick

Secretary of the Committee

Damien always interpreted this document in the broad sense. He judged that "from time to time" meant all the time; and that "the circumstances" required him to work in the interests of the lepers from morning to night, or else from night to morning.

Tribute should be paid at this point to Mr. R. W. Meyer, who was always friendly to Father Damien in his apostolate.

Meyer was a German Lutheran, prudent and firm, honest and good, untouched by prejudice. He had the qualities needed for administering the leprosarium.

Meyer and Damien showed great mutual respect and unfailing candor in their almost daily collaboration. Of course, the Catholic priest and the Lutheran official did not always see eye to eye. Their points of view were not the same and their judgments about such and such a sick person or employee sometimes collided. But both had the welfare of the lepers at heart, both were intelligent and upright, and, as the numerous letters of Meyer preserved in the Picpus archives testify, their friendship never lost its vitality.

"I need your valuable cooperation," wrote the superintendent once, "for, you know, you are the only one I really trust."

And again: "I hope your letter will succeed in cheering me up. If I were able to go out, I would be with you without delay, and we would share a time we could recall with joy."

After a year and a half at lazaretto, Damien had succeeded in clarifying and improving his position notably.

With respect to his superiors, he was the missionary regularly appointed to the apostolate on the island.

With regard to the lepers, he was the friend who would never desert them.

In the eyes of Mr. Meyer, he was a highly esteemed co-worker.

As for the Board of Health, which had at first opposed his presence on the island, that body now permitted his presence without favoring it or considering it indispensable. The time was to come when the Board—with some good and intelligent men at its head, like Premier Gibson and the Frenchman Trousseau—would look for ways and means of assisting the apostle and of establishing official relations with him.

"The government is very good to me," wrote Damien in 1879. "While the Mission furnishes me with all I require, I receive each week from the Board my allotment of food on the same basis as the sick." It may be taken for granted that Damien did not eat double portions but distributed the supplement to make others happy.

One day, he sent his aged carriage to the wagon builders at Honolulu. President Gibson heard about it and wrote:

Honolulu, December 20, 1882

Reverend and dear Father Damien,

Some days ago, you sent here for repairs the carriage which serves you at the leprosarium. It appears to me pretty well used up. Highly appreciating the services that you so faithfully render to the unfortunate lepers, the Board has authorized me to get you a new carriage. I am sending it to you, begging you to accept it with the expression of my affection and my profound esteem.

Walter M. Gibson

President of the Board of Health

In November 1877, when the position of under-superintendent fell vacant, the government urged it upon Father Damien. They offered him $10,000 a year. He replied: "You ought to offer me $100,000 a year to do what I am doing, but I would not take it. Even at that salary, if I were interested only in profits, I would not stay here five minutes. Do you think that my mother would still own me to be her son, if I yielded to accepting a salary for this kind of work?"

All that they could prevail upon him to do was to take charge until a new under-superintendent could be named.

His interim regime came to an end on February 25, 1878. Thereupon, he gave a sigh of relief. "I have been patient for three months," he wrote. "But now I am free!" That responsibility had eaten into his time. He realized, also, that a temporal administrator charged with keeping order and handing out punishments has difficulty in maintaining his popularity. He much preferred to stay within the limits of his spiritual mission.

He could not be reproached with having lined his nest out of the proceeds of his office. Instead of $3,333, which had been offered to him for his work, he was satisfied with payments of about forty dollars a month. To his superior he accounted for the use to which he put the money: "I have not put it in my purse," he wrote. "It is the chapel and the poor that have profited from it."

Chapter 9

Father to the Lepers

Among the works of mercy by which the elect will be recognized on judgment day, the catechism lists the following:

"Feeding the hungry, giving drink to the thirsty, clothing the naked, visiting the imprisoned, consoling the afflicted, converting sinners, forgiving injuries, caring for the sick, burying the dead."

Molokai gave every opportunity for living this gospel way of life. By natural inclination, as well as by firmness of will, Damien lived this way of life to the full.

He provided for the lepers food, clothing, housing, medicines and diversions. For them, he turned himself into a lawyer, a beggar, a banker, an errand boy, a nurse, a carpenter, a bandmaster, an undertaker and a policeman.

It is a rare organization that does not boast of at least a few intelligent and loyal employees. Probably Mr. Meyer's administration was blessed with some men of this kind; but most of the employees were distinctly inferior.

Damien tried to repair the damage such employees caused, to supply what their carelessness omitted, to combat their immorality, to protect at all costs the interests of the sick – in a word, to watch over all as a father watches over his children.

In the meantime, renown came his way, and opposition—with the opposition predominating; and he was as little concerned about the one as about the other. And when at length leprosy itself came to him, he welcomed it as a long awaited vehicle to carry him the rest of his journey to the grave.

The leprosarium had been in existence seven years when he took up his work there. During these first seven years, the number of colonists had fluctuated between 200 and 400. It leaped to 800 in 1873 and maintained itself thereafter with not too large a variation, as the following table indicates:

YEAR	ADMISSIONS TO LAZARETTO	DEATHS AT LAZARETTO	NUMBER OF LEPERS AT END OF THE YEAR		
			MEN	WOMEN	TOTAL
1873	415	142	515	285	800
1874	78	141	455	266	721
1875	178	149	465	279	744
1876	75	119	432	262	694
1877	122	129	433	251	684
1878	209	111	477	305	782
1879	92	204	414	254	668
1880	51	151	352	216	568
1881	195	129	398	236	634
1882	70	111	369	224	593
1883	300	150	453	290	743
1884	108	167	430	252	682
1885	103	142	422	221	643
1886	43	101	389	191	580
1887	220	111	449	239	688
1888	571	236	643	368	1011
1889	307	149	722	444	1166

This table includes only lepers. To be complete, it should also list the employees at the lazaretto and the healthy persons who accompanied their leper relatives. In the course of time, the number of these healthy relatives would amount to one hundred. The parish of Father Damien, therefore, sheltered about a thousand persons.

The statistics reveal that death was a frequent visitor at the leprosarium. But the places left empty by the dead were quickly filled by newcomers to Molokai whom the *Mokili* brought every week. That wretched boat, which traveled at six knots an hour, completed the round of the island before touching at Kalaupapa. Usually it arrived in the course of the morning, but occasionally it came at night. Father Damien never missed being at the landing place waiting for it. He would have already said his Mass, in order to be entirely at the service of the new arrivals. He would bring them coffee and hot food. Then he would take them to the grounds about his priest-house at Kalawao, keeping them at his home until lodgings had been found, doing everything in his power to brighten the first hours they had to pass on that sad shore.

Food and Clothing

For a long time the provisions of food for the lazaretto left much to be desired. The quality of the food was mediocre; the quantity, insufficient; the distribution, hardly fair.

When Damien had spent ten years at Molokai, he was still receiving from Mr. Meyer letters like the following:

> *Kalae*, February 21, 1884
>
> My dear Father Damien,
>
> I am deeply grieved to hear about the distress of the poor lepers, but I hope the *Mokili* will arrive Sunday or Monday with provisions. It is a case of *force majeure*. For several days, the boat which carries the mails has been unable to dock. This has placed me in the position of being unable to forward complaints to Honolulu.

> I haven't a cent in the bank. I am unable to get from the Board even a dollar to pay on bills already in arrears. Not only are the food ration bills for the current year unpaid, but the bills for the rations of the last six months of the year just ended are not yet settled. I am, therefore, unable to buy anything with which to replenish the store.

The store referred to belonged to the Board. Sick persons who had any money could get underwear and clothing there. But such fortunate ones were few in number. Moreover, the poor labored under many additional handicaps. For example, they had to share their food rations with their non-leper relatives, since the latter were not provided for by the Board.

Fortunately, Damien had a store of his own, where provisions were supplied gratis. He replenished the stock of his store with gifts sent by the Mission and to a great extent later on with gifts dispatched to him from other countries.

Lepers of means lived by preference at Kakanalua, midway between Kalawao and Kalaupapa. But the poor, in order to avoid long trips, managed to build their hovels at Kalawao itself, as near as possible to the marvelous storeroom of Father Damien. In that place were kept his packing-cases, his cans, his barrels and all his goods. It was a touching sight to see him surrounded by the pitiable crowd of his beloved sons and daughters, rolling up his sleeves, flashing his broad smile, giving a word of encouragement to each one, giving, giving again, giving always: bread, biscuits, rice, sugar, eggs, tobacco, sweets, even chickens when he had any.

They deceived him often enough, it appears; they told him tales he swallowed too easily; but he was not inclined to make investigations that would have chilled his charity.

His store and his charity, however, could not cover every need. Besides, it was the responsibility of the Hawaiian government and of the Board of Health to furnish the food and clothing required by the lepers.

Damien did not cease reminding them of this responsibility, sometimes in prudent words, sometimes in rather forceful language. He drew up grievances in proper form; he denounced ill-made appropriations; he dealt out many pieces of advice, congratulations and encouragement, as well as outlines of projects—all with the men in mind in whose hands lay the destiny of his children. He made his influence felt as widely as he was permitted; and as the years passed, he was given more and more latitude. Was he not proving to be the best friend of the lepers, their representative, their spokesman? Had he not identified himself with them? "We lepers...," he used to say well in advance of the day when he knew he had become one; and he said the words whether he spoke to the lepers or about them.

Nowhere does his role appear in better light than in the report he drew up in 1886 at the request of Mr. Gibson.

To read this important document intelligently, one must note the stage at which it was written and recall that the situation described in it bears little resemblance to that of the preceding years.

Damien pleaded first for good rations:

"The food a leper eats has a great effect on his disease. Hawaiian taro, valuable as flour and very digestible, is the best food for us. I have never found that it had any harmful effects even in the course of bouts with fever and other ailments to which our sick are subject. Kanaka lepers cannot do without it. A dozen years ago, when they were deprived of it for three months, many died and a great many others went into decline, despite the fact that potatoes and rice were on hand in quantity.

"As the Board provides for us every week six to seven hundred rations of taro, I shall offer some suggestions as to the best way of getting it to us.

"We procure it from the natives in the southern part of the island. Since the barrier-cliffs of the Pali make transportation by land impossible, it must come to us by sea, whether it is unprocessed or is in the form of *poi*. It comes on barges, on sailing schooners, or on steamers. I hasten to inform you that our people much prefer the steamers, for the reason that barges and schooners do not get here when the sea is either windless or too rough. Our community is then deprived of its good *poi*, which proceeds to spoil at its source without benefit to anyone.

"In default of *poi*, we have stores of rice and of biscuits. But, I repeat, it is only the Chinese that can live on a steady diet of rice without detriment.

"We also have, in case of absolute want, some sweet potatoes that our lepers have managed to raise despite their maimed hands. From these, the Hawaiians succeed in distilling a highly intoxicating liquor of which they are very fond. In this connection, I am happy to send my sincere thanks to the Board for its wise enactment forbidding the use of this liquor at the lazaretto.

"In addition to the solid food, a pint of fresh milk a day would be most beneficial to the lepers. But where can we get enough milk for so many people? If I may, I recommend to the Board with all the energy at my command the project of increasing as much as possible the size of our herd of good cows. We have excellent pasturage here to sustain them. Unfortunately, the size of our herd has greatly diminished in recent times. Beef cattle have been coming to us so slowly that our cows have had to be slaughtered. Remember that 5,000 pounds of meat are required here each week! The result is that we lack sufficient milk. I regret to say that for several years none of our lepers, except those in the hospital, have been able to have any milk. May I urge you to solicit from the new legislature funds for dispatching here in one shipment as many head of cattle as our plain can nourish—that is to say, between five hundred and a thousand. If this were to be done, we should never lack either milk or meat. The sick would profit by this arrangement at no cost to the Board."

The question of clothing was also very serious: "In winter, the climate at the lazaretto is rather cold, and at certain stages in its development leprosy retards the circulation of the blood. Indeed, our lepers often complain of the cold. Those who have warm clothing are better able to throw off the chill. But the others are afflicted with fever and coughs; their faces and limbs swell; disease then attacks their lungs and carries them swiftly to the grave."

Damien then glanced back several years:

"When I arrived at the lazaretto, the greatest number of the lepers lacked suitable garments. Each year, the Board provided for each of them a new garment and a pair of sheets; but, either through negligence or through slovenliness, after a few months almost all of them were without linen and were running about in tatters.

"Water was scarce; and the sick wallowed in frightful dirt. The stench of their sweat and their filth was at first insupportable. It took me a long time to accustom myself to it. How many times, when I was performing my priestly duties at their side, I was forced to hold my nose and even to run outside to catch a breath of fresh air! Their emanations caused such itching in the skin of my legs that I had to wear high boots to prevent it. The stench so impregnated my clothes that I had to smoke a pipe to counteract it.

"At present, thanks to the store, the situation is better. May I be permitted to observe, however, that six dollars a year is absolutely insufficient to allow each leper to furnish himself with linen and clothing."

As a result of this protest, the Board increased the grant to ten dollars. As usual, it was upon Damien's initiative and in accordance with his planning that the Board also laid down a line of piping to bring water to the lazaretto so that the sick had the means of cleaning their linen and of washing themselves. Damien acted as a water carrier for those who were too infirm to go to the taps themselves.

Housing and Public Works

Before Damien's time, all the lepers outside of a few wealthy ones lived huddled in hovels—huts made of boughs—that were mean, damp and unsanitary.

Toward the end of 1874, a winter hurricane swept away half of them. Many of the sick were left without shelter and had to sleep out in the open, shivering under wet blankets and lying on grass mattresses that had been turned by their own filth into so many dung hills.

Damien informed Mr. Meyer, who without delay gathered up materials to repair the damage. Schooners arrived, loaded with beams and planks. They also brought some carpenters, but these refused to build without being paid. Once again the veteran church-builder had to exercise his skill in the interest of the poor. "I lend them my arms for several days, and lo! they are housed!" he wrote.

It was the first time that decent housing appeared at the lazaretto. Damien constructed large numbers of little, white-washed wooden cabins. At his request, the government later followed suit by erecting a good number, beginning in 1878. As late as 1888, James Sinnet—one of the lay volunteers who came to help on Molokai during Damien's last months on earth—found the Father, "under a tropical sun, covered with sweat and dust, hewing and nailing, and raising cabins in the midst of his lepers."

He did duty for the helpless, he assisted the others, he urged everyone to get a decent house: "With the objective of providing themselves with one, many families have put aside what had been allotted them for the clothing that was less urgent at the moment than a house; and they have entrusted me with their little savings. I am confident of the approval of the Board; and I ask you to send me the lumber, nails, tacks and paint, a detailed order for which you will find enclosed herewith...." He was the banker of the poor, then; he drew up plans for them; he gave orders in their name; and with their help or without it, he built their little houses.

"Be careful not to catch that vile disease!" Father Modeste had counseled him. Damien did not follow this advice to the letter. He took off his cassock, set up his carpenter's bench in the midst of the lepers and worked with them like a skilled mechanic surrounded by his apprentices, passing to them and receiving back from them his mallets, hammers, chisels, rules and dividers without any worry about contagion. Should he have told them they were infectious? What mattered was not that one should guard against disease, but that all one's children should be well housed.

Since the number of the lepers was on the increase, the Board decided to settle some of them at Kalaupapa. Three or four mud huts straggling along a dangerous landing beach: that was the original Kalaupapa. A "government road," really only a wretched path, connected this landing place with Kalawao. Father Damien undertook to make this "port" more accessible by widening the path into a usable road; and for this project he was engineer, works-foreman, treasurer/paymaster and laborer. "Your Excellency," he wrote to the Minister of the Interior on July 31, 1883, "we have begun to repair the government road at the leprosarium. At this half-way point in the accomplishment of the work, I beg you to be good enough to send me the sum due up to the present, in order to encourage the workmen to continue the enterprise."

The sum failed to arrive speedily. Damien waited only eight days before dunning the minister again and pressing home the necessity for broadening his public works program:

> Sir,
>
> Last January, I was charged by your late predecessor with the task of repairing the government road from

Kalawao to Kalaupapa. It was understood that I was to receive $300 for this work. Will you be so kind as to send me what is due as of today; namely, $152.20?

And this is not all. You know the dangerous rocks that lie off the landing-stage. Mr. Meyer and I have just gone down to look them over. It would require dynamite to remove them. I know a man at Halava who could undertake this job. Do you wish to have me talk it over with him? I should also require some barrels of cement.

Sincerely yours,
Damien, Catholic Priest

The road was finished; the rocks were removed; and in its turn, Kalaupapa was covered with little white houses, each with its flower garden.

Work and Play

Father Damien's report also deals with work and leisure: "Formerly, very few lepers did any work; today, the greater number cultivate potato fields. They keep the harvest for themselves, and this permits them to give up some of their food ration in return for cash. Some of them even sell their surplus potatoes to the administration, which is quite ready to buy them when bad weather prevents the steamer from landing with the regular rations."

It was Father Damien who persuaded the sick to take up agriculture and the Board to purchase their little crops.

He encouraged everyone to become a landowner, to raise flowers, to buy a horse, to play music. He organized festivals, multiplied diversions and arranged processions and public games.

Dull idleness vanished and with it many vices. The

Kanakas, so fond of music and lively merrymaking, had rediscovered the joy of life.

Horse racing was very much to their taste. "I assure you," Damien says in his report with some relish, "nine-tenths of the able-bodied lepers now devote themselves to it, whereas hitherto scarcely a tenth enjoyed this blessing. It is a pastime with most beneficial effects upon us since, by stimulating the circulation of the blood, it slows down the progress of the disease and mitigates its pains."

Music was needed to give rhythm to these pastimes. There was talent aplenty, but instruments were lacking, save at first a few drums. From some old cans, Father Damien fashioned some small pipes and flutes. Later, he used some timely alms to purchase coronets, bugles, clarinets, trombones and a bassdrum. Fully equipped with these instruments, the band delighted in pouring floods of harmony over the gatherings on the beach. According to Dutton—the lay volunteer who shared Fr. Damien's last days and remained among the lepers of Molokai for the rest of his own life—Father Damien himself found great pleasure in listening to it.

People were soon speaking about this innovation. "I must not forget," wrote a visitor in 1876, "the serenade that was given for us on Thursday evening in the moonlight. After supper, we stepped out to take a stroll in the cool air. A hundred lepers were waiting for us with large flags, four drums and a dozen other musical instruments. For two whole hours, a great variety of pieces was played to perfection by those musicians, some of whom lacked all but two or three fingers or had lips swollen by the disfiguring process of leprosy."

When the members of the band grew tired of blowing on their brasses, the choral group stepped out to spell them. For Father Damien also encouraged vocal arts, and his singers won as much applause as his instrumentalists.

"During certain numbers played by the band," said

Dutton, "I have seen a musician lose a finger from his hand and another lose a piece of his lip; but they continued to play nevertheless. As for the leper woman who presided at the harmonium in 1886, when she no longer had any fingers save those on her right hand, she made a piece of wood serve in place of those missing from her left, and with this makeshift arrangement played the accompaniment on the bass notes."

The Priest-house

The grounds about the priest-house at Kalawao were used for these festivals and gatherings.

In his first days on the island, we have seen Damien, without any priest-house, eating and sleeping under the broad leaves of a great pandanus tree.

His benefactors in Honolulu, however, were not slow in sending him the materials for building a cabin five yards long by four wide. He finished it in eight days and lived in it for five years.

In 1878, he received permission from his provincial to erect a "real priest-house which would cost from fifty to sixty dollars." It measured eight yards by seven and had a second story to which a flight of outside steps gave access. "Nothing could be more suitable," he wrote to the provincial. "If one of my friends from Tremeloo came to see me, I would be able to put him up," he said in a letter to his mother.

That same letter to his aged mother gave some details calculated to reassure her:

"I live alone. Don't worry. The lepers do not come into my home. As for my meals, I have only two a day, and the woman who prepares them is not sick. In the morning, I take some rice, meat, coffee and pancakes. In the evening, I eat whatever was left over from the earlier meal with a cup of tea that I heat on my lamp. You can see that I do not suffer from hunger and that I even live in good style. My poultry yard furnishes me all the eggs I need. As for the rest, I am so busy that I am seldom in the house. I must even steal some hours from sleep in order to write to you."

At times, then, Damien had a cook who was not a leper. But there were other times when he had to turn to lepers for his cooks; however, he ordered them to wear gloves at their task.

Doctors

For several years, the isolated victims on Molokai had not been provided with any doctors. To all appearances they were regarded as incurables whose lives it was useless to prolong. It was only in 1878 that the matter was given any thought. Even then, the position of doctor on Molokai left much to be desired, and it is not surprising to find the incumbents succeeding one another rapidly. At first, they did not reside on the island in constant attendance upon the sick. They put in occasional appearances, remained a few days and went away. Two or three weeks would elapse before their return.

That fashion of interpreting the practice of medicine aroused the anger of the sensible Mr. Meyer:

"It is pure comedy!" he wrote in 1884. "It is a device for enabling us to say that a doctor is provided for the leprosarium. When doctors are needed, they are not at hand. The simplest drugs cannot be had. The more I see these doctors at work, the less helpful I find them for our sick people. I rebel against such a system! Let a doctor remain here in residence, or let them stay away altogether!"

Until the arrival of Father Damien, then, the sick had been almost completely neglected. They had at their disposal only some native drugs, some of them harmless, others dangerous. They went about without linen or cotton-wool to cover their ulcers, which were thus exposed to dust, to flies and to vermin.

And when the slightest complication set in, they died for want of a remedy that might have relieved them and postponed their premature death.

Under these circumstances, Damien took on his shoulders the work of hospital attendant and doctor. He visited all the lepers at least once a week. It was always a frightful spectacle that met his eyes.

"Half of the sick," he wrote, "are living corpses that worms have begun to devour, first inside, then outside, leaving horrible sores for the most part beyond the possibility of relief."

Damien began his daily circuit by going through the hospital; then he walked from cabin to cabin, his pockets loaded with remedies, sedatives and whatever else he thought would be helpful.

His smiling face, his cheerful and encouraging words, and the kindness of his heart diffused optimism, consolation and at times even joy. His not-over-refined disposition made the simple hearted Kanakas feel at home with him, for he seemed to be one of them. Long since had he abolished the barrier that could have separated him from those he once called "savages."

He ignored the putrefaction all around him. He knelt at the side of a dying leper stretched on a grass mat soiled with filth; he alleviated his final anguish; he helped him to die well. He sat on the ground near a sick man, chatting with him, taking interest in all his concerns, applying the best remedies at hand, offering the sweets he had brought with him, assuring the sufferer that he would hurry back again at the first sign of danger and that he would under no circumstances abandon him.

For the more able-bodied lepers who wished to care for the helpless, Damien laid down a set of directives and furnished suggestions for medical assistance and morale-building. But if none of these volunteers was near, he good-humoredly took upon himself the job of sweeping, scrubbing, washing the linen and putting the wretched house in order.

The line in his letter to his mother: "I eat at my house only in the morning and in the evening," is explained by the fact that at noon he was always busy on his rounds. The lepers, of course, invited him to share their food. Without the slightest sign of repugnance, he ate with them the family *poi* served in a common gourd, and at the conclusion of the meal smoked in his turn the pipe which, in accordance with the Kanaka custom, was passed from mouth to mouth.

Was this heroism? Had the revulsion of his earlier days disappeared?

"I have seen him dress the most loathsome sores as if he were arranging flowers," said one eye-witness.

To a leper in the last stages of the disease who begged him to take greater precautions, Damien replied: "Do not be disturbed, my son. Even if the disease siezes my body, God is going to give me another on Resurrection Day. Is not the all-important thing the saving of one's soul?"

Along with Father Damien, there had come to the lazaretto a man named Williamson who had contracted Hansen's disease while nursing lepers. He was a former doctor's assistant at Kahili, where he had had considerable experience. He was placed in charge of the sick at the hospital; and he taught Father Damien all he knew.

Damien studied hard, applied himself assiduously and acquired a remarkable skill. From 1874 to 1878 he was, to all practical purposes, the only doctor at the leprosarium. After that period had passed, he worked with the regular doctors, perfected his skills more and more, and obtained some excellent results. With scrupulous care, he prepared potions, disinfected sores and bandaged or amputated gangrenous limbs.

Dr. Woods, a medical inspector in the American Navy, gave this evidence, a copy of which was kept by the government at Honolulu:

"I made a trip of inspection to Molokai. There was no

longer a resident physician there. I admired the patience with which the good Father Damien lavished his affectionate care on the lepers and the completely scientific method he followed in treating them. Having visited all the places on earth where leprosy is endemic, I can testify that in no other part of the world are the lepers so happy and so well cared for as in the Hawaiian Islands."

Mr. Meyer also applauded the skill of his friend:

"While we were still without a doctor, it was the good Father Damien who cared for the lepers. I certify that the mortality was not higher in that period than it is today and that our sick endured their distress and their chronic ailments with no less comfort."

Our doctor without diploma did not confine himself to prudently applying the remedies then in fashion; he moved heaven and earth to discover better ones. He who no longer found time to write to his relatives, sent long letters to the ends of the earth to get some new drug that people had told him about.

In 1876, he put his confidence in *Rayne's Pills*: "Send me some dozens of boxes," he wrote to Dr. Kibbin at Honolulu. "These pills, to which we have become accustomed, do us more good than any other purgative."

In 1878, he heard people talking about *Hoang-Nan Pills*. It was Chinese remedy extracted from a species of reddish ivy containing a subtle poison. To Father Etienne, a Dominican at Trinidad, he wrote:

"I received with joy beyond words the box of *Hoang-Nan* pills as well as your friendly letter so full of encouragement and confidence. I read it in translation to a large audience of lepers, whom it filled with joy and hope. They have discussed the matter and raised a subscription to purchase *Hoang-Nan* in quantity. I myself have tried it out on a good Catholic who is much improved through its use.

"Out of pity for my beloved sick, who all call me their *Makna* (father), and who suffer indescribable torment, in the name of Our Lord Jesus Christ, who healed lepers, I entreat you to send me a supply of this medication by the most direct route, with the utmost speed and without regard for expense. Bear in mind that my need for it is proportionate to the considerable number of my leper children. I will reimburse you for all your expenses through our mother House in Paris...."

After fifteen months, he gave an account of the results achieved:

"I did not wish to write you sooner, for I wanted to be sure that the improvements due to your providential medication would be lasting. It has prolonged the lives of many; it has restored to others the use of their limbs.

"In six months we have been administering it on a wide scale, and its reputation has continued to grow....

"I hope that the Board of Health will adopt it. My supply will last, I think, till April. That is when the chambers (of the Hawaiian Parliament) come into session. If the Board does act, I shall get my friends in Parliament to intervene, for the purpose of persuading the government to decide in favor of purchasing some *Hoang-Nan*...."

The Children

Among his patients, the children were the apple of his eye. Visitors have described these small victims, these little ones snatched from mothers' arms to be set down on this melancholy shore where leprosy would complete its work of steadily defiling and devouring their innocent flesh. If their parents had been permitted to see them again, they would not have recognized these deformed dwarfs.

Far removed from the affection of their natural protectors, these unhappy youngsters were adopted by Damien. He took the place of both father and mother – to love them, to protect them, to give them the most tender care. In 1883, he sent to his bishop the roster of his "forty-four adopted children." They constituted his real home and family, in whose bosom Father Damien spent most of his time and tasted most of his consolations. He liked to have the children around him, in the neighborhood of his priest-house, on the grounds of the Mission. Here he founded an orphanage for girls and later an asylum or boys' home for the lads.

"I have a small orphanage for young leper girls," he wrote in 1888, "for whom an elderly woman who is not a leper acts as mother and cook. We have a common kitchen and share our rations. We consider ourselves well fed. We have planted a large field of potatoes, which keep in good condition underground and form our reserve against the time when rations do not arrive as expected. Some charitable souls send us clothing, which often come to me through the kindness of the mother superior at Honolulu."

There was a boys' school to which Father Damien used to go to give religious instruction. Under pretext of neutrality toward religion, the Board of Health stopped him. Thereupon he built for these little lepers an asylum that was a replica of the girls' orphanage. It was housed in two buildings—the one about a dozen yards from his priest-house and the other about eighteen yards distant.

The inmates were so well nourished, washed, cared for and nursed that candidates for admission exceeded the facilities. Even adults who had neither funds nor friends begged for admission. Nor did Father Damien have the heart to send away all of these latter.

This project was a heavy drain on his already flattened resources, for he had to find remuneration for the able-bodied lepers who worked for him there. In order to meet his expenses, he hit upon clever fund-raising schemes, which Mr. Meyer countenanced with a smile: he begged far and wide; he went from door to door accompanied by some of his orphans; he raised potatoes, cabbages and other vegetables and by selling them made some money.

Poor little orphans! All ill, hideous, deformed; but all happy in the bosom of that large family governed by the best of fathers.

Having been knocked about from pillar to post before arriving at Molokai, many of these orphans still carried the names given to them by caprice or scorn. Some were called John, Damien or Peter, after the priest who happened to baptize them; others rejoiced in names like these: Waterbird, Eyes-of-fire, Window, Morgue, Heaven-has-spoken, Seated-out-in-the-cold, Vomitory, Rat-eater, Pigsty, Atlantic Ocean, River of Truth.

Damien saw only their fine points. "They learn their catechism well," he wrote, "and they assist at Mass and benediction. Now that I have become a sort of doctor, somewhat like my patron saint, I try to alleviate their sufferings. You may think that it is distressing to live in the midst of beings so repulsive. Really, they spell happiness for me."

From another letter: "The day before yesterday, upon returning from an errand, I came upon one of my little leper girls, who asked me to bring her Holy Viaticum without delay. The acts of thanksgiving after Communion were scarcely finished, when she gave her soul to God. Yesterday, with my own hands I made her coffin and dug her grave."

Many were those who died penniless at Molokai. In order to keep them from being buried in an ordinary blanket, Damien used to make their coffins himself. Abbé Conrardy is the authority for saying that Damien constructed about 1,600 coffins; in addition, he very often dug the graves to receive them.

Chapter 10

A Model Parish

"Not by bread alone does man live," said Jesus. To avoid spiritual hunger, man must have faith and hope. When he is in good health, he often gives little thought to the things of eternity; but sickness makes him take stock of himself and put things in order for the life beyond the grave.

Damien, who had become a missionary to save souls, found at Molokai the means of fulfilling his apostolic vows to the letter. In that place, with one foot already in the grave, lived seven to eight hundred unfortunates, face to face with approaching death and eternity. Every year, twenty percent of them died. Without fear of having his zeal misunderstood, the apostle could speak to them of the judgment of God, of Christ the Redeemer and of the Virgin Most Merciful. He had an ever-present opportunity to baptize, convert, absolve those at the point of death, give hope to the distressed and bring shipwrecked souls to the port of salvation.

On the balance sheet his spiritual deeds equal his corporal works of charity. He succeeded in turning the lazaretto into a flourishing center of Christian living.

Does he deserve all the credit for this achievement? There can be little doubt of it when one considers the number of well-intentioned co-workers sent to him and the short time they managed to stay at the task. In all, Damien worked without a helper for nine years.

From his arrival in May, 1873, to February, 1874, his parish covered the whole island of Molokai.

From February, 1874, to July, 1878, his parish was restricted to the lazaretto itself. The southern part of the island with its two hundred Catholics scattered among two thousand natives had been placed under the charge of Father Andreas Burgerman. From July, 1878, to June, 1880, Father Burgerman lived at Kalaupapa, and the care of the southern district which he had left fell once again on Father Damien's shoulders.

In June 1880, Father Burgerman disappeared. For the ensuing fifteen months Damien had charge of the entire island.

On September 8, 1881, another sick man, Father Albert Montiton, landed at the lazaretto. He took quarters at Kalaupapa and lived there until February, 1885.

Thereupon, Father Damien returned to his original solitude. In May, 1888, Abbé Conrardy came to his side and stayed with him to the end.

Co-workers

To judge the quality of the assistance Damien received from his intermittent co-workers, it will suffice to introduce them.

We shall speak of Abbé Conrardy at the proper time. The other three were Picpus Fathers worn down by illness.

In his lifetime, Father Burgerman certainly enjoyed the achievements which charitable Father Jourdan has recognized; but he also had grave disabilities beyond common understanding.

He was a Hollander and was forty-seven years old when he fell victim to elephantiasis in Tahiti. He was passionately fond of the practice of medicine, and was succeeding notably in that field when he got the idea of becoming under-superintendent of the leprosarium at Molokai. He went through phases that caused much trouble for his superiors.

At first, Damien passed favorable judgment on him; he took him for some time as his confessor. Later on, however, Damien wrote to the general: "Send me a good son of the Congregation, not an obstinate gentleman." With the approval of his superiors, he declined any longer to confess to him. He suffered deeply from having the man as companion for two years.

At the end of his stay at Kalaupapa, Father Burgerman no longer greeted his confrere. When Damien died and material for his biography was being assembled, the Hollander was still unappeased and was reluctant to reply to inquiries. He ended his life, however, in the best of dispositions and deserved thereby the gratifying obituary article printed in the annals of his congregation.

Father Albert was quite different. He was a fervent priest who had done excellent work among the Kanakas of Tahiti. His success there was attributed in part to his musical talent, which he displayed chiefly with the clarinet and the harmonium. He was aware of his uncommon ability, but disease had sorely tried him. He, too, had contracted elephantiasis in the islands of Oceania. It was diagnosed as Hansen's disease, and he was placed in quarantine at Molokai, which he was forbidden to leave.

With the prestige lent by a successful career and a seniority of fifteen years over Damien, he arrived from Rome, where, after having made a lecture trip through France, he had been received by Leo XIII. Somewhere on the way he had been told that the leper priest lacked judgment and needed a guardian. He had even heard infamous rumors concerning his chastity, calumnies which he blurted out to Damien, thus souring their relations at the very start. Damien nevertheless pardoned him without delay.

These two men of such decided character did not always see eye to eye. The fault was primarily on the part of the newcomer, if one should use the word "fault" in connection with an old campaigner wasted and embittered by disease. Before Father Albert joined Father Damien on Molokai, the vice-provincial wrote to the superior general: "We have had here in Honolulu for a month Father Albert, who runs after everyone and from whom everyone tries to escape. He is a pitiable mischief-maker who cannot get along with anyone. The doctor, I believe, is going to relieve us of him next week and send him back to Molokai." Later, the vice-provincial wrote that Father Albert was "no longer of any use but to be the confessor of Father Damien." But Father Albert, who lived in memories of the past, did not see his role in that light. He interfered in everything, made no concessions at all and aspired to play the role of director.

"He is unbearable," wrote Damien right after Albert's arrival on the scene. That view was shared by everyone. The bishop of Honolulu was of the same opinion: "Father Albert has talent, zeal and many virtues. But he is choleric and wants his own way too much. He has never been able to live in peace, either with his superiors or with outsiders."

What Damien put up with during the more than three years Father Albert spent with him can be imagined. In 1882, the situation became so intolerable that, at the very limit of his endurance, Father Damien accepted the idea of separation from his beloved lepers. "Seeing that Father Albert does not care for me," he wrote to his bishop, "and that he has an impossible disposition, I turn to you to decide what I ought to do. I am quite willing to leave Molokai, if that is the will of God."

"Quite willing...." This was another way of saying he was ready to suffer martyrdom.

Nevertheless, Damien did more than his share under the circumstances. He granted his confrere every possible favor, constructed a church for him and took care of his sick and even of his vegetable garden.

On April 28, 1885, the vice-provincial totaled up the balance sheet of the activities of Father Albert at Molokai: "Except for the children that he baptized and the sick he attended at the point of death, this poor Father has accomplished only trifles here."

However, Father Albert had his good points. Believing himself to be almost cured, he asked of his own volition to quit Molokai, and he set off to use up his last ounces of strength in Tahiti. By way of farewell to his long-suffering neighbor, he wryly wrote: "Good-bye! I do not bear you any grudge for all the trouble I have caused you."

Damien, who esteemed him and loved him and by virtue of patience had finally succeeded in adjusting to him, wept copiously at his departure. Damien had become sick himself; he feared he would never be able to get off the island again; and he dreaded a future without a confessor. "I beg you not to take Father Albert from me," he wrote to the bishop on February 2, 1885. And he gave his reasons:

"1. I am disabled for life. I drag my leg as I walk. When I go to the hospital, which is only five minutes from here, I am so exhausted as to groan all the following night from pain. 2. If actually I have become a leper, my death is not far off. I do not intend to be excessively preoccupied with my body; I must be concerned about my soul and, thus, I must have a good confessor at hand. Now the spiritual direction of Father Albert has served me well and I should be happy to profit by it until I am on my deathbed...."

For his part, Father Albert had been with his confrere too

long to fail to understand him. He never spoke of him but in terms of the highest admiration, and he took every opportunity to defend him against his calumniators.

In order to make the story complete, let us note that in November, 1887, another Picpus priest, Father Gregory, came to the lazaretto. The Board of Health, acting officially, had committed him there. This priest was in the last stage of Hansen's disease when he arrived; and he rendered to his confrere no other service than that of confessor. After spending three months there, he went away to die in the hospital at Kakaako.

Practically speaking, then, the religious transformation of the leprosarium was the work of Father Damien.

When Damien arrived in 1873, out of seven hundred and fifty lepers, a third were Catholic. Counting the healthy persons and putting the figure a bit high, he wrote soon after his arrival: "I judge that we have almost four hundred Catholics or catechumens. The enlargement of St. Philomena's chapel is urgent.... Be generous, then, Your Excellency; Molokai has awaited long enough to deserve your immediate assistance. As for the labor, I take that on myself; you know how I like to work as a carpenter."

Aided by his cripples, he transformed Brother Bertrand's chapel by joining a transept to it.

It was too much to ask the faithful at Kalaupapa to drag themselves three miles up to Kalawao. In 1875, Damien erected for them a well-made plank chapel. It was ten yards long, five and a half wide and seven high. In later years Father Albert put his lasting stamp on it by painting it in gaudy colors. His motley color scheme threw the Kanakas into raptures.

In 1883, a cemetery was also a prime necessity at Kalaupapa. At the request of Father Albert, Damien undertook the task, but his work was not appreciated: "Father Albert is difficult," he wrote. "I have made his cemetery the best I was capable of doing. For the entrance gate, he wanted something elaborate.... When it was almost completed, he turned it down. And as I was unwilling to make him another, here he is now very much nettled and threatens not to take my place at Kalawao on Sundays when I have to go into the South."

In the beginning, that southern part of the island did not have any chapels. Damien attended to the matter in the course of the year 1874. For Father Burgerman, who was then in charge of the Catholics of that district, he built in four months: four wooden chapels, a priest-house and a school. During all that time, Father Burgerman had taken his place at Kalawao.

Never, in the following years, did Damien stay away from the lazaretto for so long a time. Obliged to go to Honolulu once or twice a year, he traveled directly and remained there only three or four days. It has been calculated that in sixteen years his absences, when totaled up, scarcely covered a period equal to six months.

Life within the Parish

Father Damien did a great deal of preaching. He preached in his churches, in his houses of prayer, in his orphanages, on the grounds of his priest-house and in the huts of the lepers. According to the place and circumstance, his preaching was variously called sermon, discourse, homily, instruction, catechism, or plain conversation. On Sundays and feast days, he spoke at Mass and at benediction; each weekday morning, he gave a catechetical instruction after his Mass; in the course of the day, he visited the sick at the hospital; then he went from hut to hut, bringing into the homes teaching, exhortation or reprimand.

"Upon entering a house, I always offer first the remedy that heals souls. Those who decline it do not meet the slightest discrimination in my distribution of bodily aids and comforts. I make myself a leper among lepers to win all to Christ. When I preach, I am accustomed to say: 'We other people, the lepers....' Except for some reluctant non-Catholics, all look upon me as their father. Usually I receive respectful attention when I speak. My tone varies according to circumstances. Sometimes, I bring only consolation and gentle words; sometimes I mix in a little acid and vinegar to waken bad consciences; sometimes I must thunder and threaten the impenitent with eternal punishment."

He kept a notebook for jotting down outlines of his sermons. They are based chiefly on passages of Scripture, upon which he made comments suitable to the Kanaka mentality and practical applications to the local situation. Here is a sample:

"The earth is only a place of temporary exile. Heaven is our true country, which we others, the lepers, are assured of entering soon. There we shall receive compensation for our sufferings. There will be no more hideous leprosy or pain. We shall be transfigured, happy and beautiful in proportion to our patience in bearing our trials here below."

It will be remembered that at Kohala he had trained some "prayer leaders." He had many of them at Molokai, to give the sick the opportunity of prayer in common in the vicinity of their homes.

"On Sunday afternoons we have, for the less active lepers, meetings directed by my prayer leaders. Four or five houses at Kalawao are thronged to the bursting point. As for me, after saying Mass, administering baptisms, and gulping down my lunch, I set out for Kalaupapa, where I have three meetings scheduled: one for healthy natives, the second for lepers in the vicinity of the landing place, the third for those at the point of the promontory."

He made many conversions and administered more than a hundred baptisms a year. Every able-bodied Catholic could get to Mass on Sundays. Many came to Mass every morning and took part every evening in the recitation of the Rosary in the chapel. The lepers had a special devotion to the Way of the

Cross and to Our Lady, Comforter of the Afflicted. Many of them could be seen walking the fourteen stations of the sorrowful way leading from the Pretorium to Calvary; and, with the coming of the month of Mary, they used to decorate with flowers the altar of the Blessed Virgin. Almost all wore the rosary around their necks. At least three hundred of them went to Communion every week.

No visitor was unimpressed by the fervor of the observance of Sundays on Molokai.

The highlight of the day was High Mass at St. Philomena's. The church tastefully adorned, the altar bright with candles and flowers, the many choir boys in red cassocks and lace surplices, the music, the singing, community prayers recited aloud by everyone, the dignity and gentleness of the celebrant, the true father of his leprous family calling down God's blessing on them—all this, on that speck of land set in a vast ocean, constituted a spectacle which fascinated Kanakas and brought tears to the eyes of visitors from the world outside.

Clifford—an English gentleman who read of Damien in the press during his last years and visited him—speaks of the sacred chanting that he heard:

"These lepers have music in their souls," he wrote. "One of them, a baritone, sang a duet with a boy whose high, clear voice made an agreeable contrast to his. A woman who in former days had played in Honolulu, drew beautiful strains from the harmonium as she passed over its keyboard hands gnawed by leprosy. The *Adeste Fideles* was excellently rendered by the boys. But my heart was most deeply touched when the choir of women sang a beautiful lament composed by a Hawaiian poet, the *By the Rivers of Babylon* of the lepers."

Damien wrote to Pamphile: "On Sunday, at High Mass, my boys sing like accomplished musicians. Unfortunately, death and tuberculosis have just taken from me the most beautiful voices in my choral group."

Stoddard, who had paid his first visit to the lazaretto in 1867, returned to it in 1884. He, too, assisted at Mass at Kalawao.

"Father had placed me to the left of the altar in the place usually reserved for him, surrounded by a little railing. "I missed nothing of the spectacle. The sacred vessels are of gold, admirably embellished. They are the gift of the pastor of St. Roch in Paris and they are used only at High Mass. All the choir boys were disfigured by leprosy. It was painful to look at some of them. Most of them no longer had fingers on their hands or toes on their feet.

"With gentle gravity, the priest began. The chapel was filled with faithful, who joined in the singing with fervor and compunction. What a contrast! At the altar bright with lights and decorations, the priest in perfect health, singing in a clear and sonorous voice the Preface and the Our Father. At his feet, acolytes with childish features marked by death. In the nave, an assemblage in which no face could be looked at without horror. The air was tainted; a fetid odor arose from those unfortunates who prayed so well. And I said to myself that such prayers, mounting to heaven through the mediation of such a servant of God, could not fail to be granted."

Stoddard spent another day in the company of Father Damien.

"His appearance was scarcely stylish," he wrote; "his cassock was worn and faded; his hair tumbled like a schoolboy's, his hands stained and hardened by toil; but the glow of health was in his face, the buoyancy of youth in his manner; while his ringing laugh, his ready sympathy and his inspiring magnetism told of one who in any sphere might do a noble work. He overrode our protestations and obliged us to share his lunch. In the evening he prepared with his own hands an excellent dinner of eggs, meat, rice and coffee.

"Between times, we accompanied him on his visits to the

sick at Kalawao. He knew all his lepers familiarly, as well as the stage of their disease. On coming to the bedside, he took up their hand to feel the pulse. No matter what their religion, they all shared his kindnesses. He spoke at some length to each of them. It was difficult, however, to get him to talk about himself. But he did mention his distress over the absence of a confessor."

The stench that distressed Stoddard, and indeed all visitors, Damien had trained himself to ignore. "I have had great difficulty bringing myself to it," he wrote, "but now I am no longer bothered by it. It is only when I am ministering to the sick whose sores are crawling with worms that I still experience malaise. These worms are like the worms that eat corpses in graves. Recently, after I had given the last sacraments to a poor man, I came home staggering like a drunkard, so greatly had the foul odor of his breath affected my brain. May these acts of mortification be efficacious enough to win from God the grace of repentance for sinners. Sometimes, also, I am thrown off balance somewhat in administering the anointing of the sick when the feet and hands of the patient are nothing but huge sores. It is a sign of approaching death."

They gave up their spirit in the arms of Father Damien. "Almost all," he wrote, "wish to die as Catholics. I have even administered baptism to a number of non-Catholic leaders at the point of death. I do all that I can to prepare everyone for a happy death; it is in that work that I find my chief consolation."

He remembered the good effects that had been wrought on him by the Redemptorist Fathers' mission years before at Braine-le-Comte. On four different occasions, he arranged for similar exercises for the benefit of his faithful.

"To make it easier for the infirm," said one of the missionaries, "we preached every day at four different places; at Kalaupapa, at the hospital, at the Church of St. Philomena and on the plain that used to be called 'the Village of Madmen,' an allusion to the orgies which took place there formerly. It is now called 'Niniveh' as a tribute to the good behavior of the converts who are there at present.

"I give up trying to express the sentiments felt in speaking before such audiences. Those who had spoken before me had burst into tears. It was only at the expense of great effort that I managed to keep the tears back.

"On the last day of the mission, I went to Kalaupapa to give the closing sermon. A cavalcade of thirty horsemen formed an escort of honor for me. Upon arriving, I found the chapel invaded by so many non-Catholics that many Catholics had to yield their regular places and remain out-of-doors. I found just enough open space on the altar steps to plant my feet."

Every parish has some parishioners who are exceptionally fervent. Usually these people are organized into formal or informal societies. The lepers' parish, too, had its confraternities: four of them.

There was the Society of Perpetual Adoration, whose members, relieving one another every half hour, formed a continual guard of honor for Jesus in the Eucharist. "Sometimes," wrote Damien, "their infirmities keep them from taking their turn on guard. But at the appointed time, they substitute a half hour of recollection and prayer on their beds of pain. Our brothers and sisters of the Congregation of Picpus will be happy to know that they have rivals among the lepers, and they will welcome as associates these poor people who imitate them so faithfully."

In addition, there were three confraternities of a charitable nature. The first, the Holy Childhood, banded together young people and children; the second, composed of men, was under the patronage of St. Joseph, and its members pledged themselves to visit the sick in their homes; the third united the women under the protection of the Blessed Virgin in order to bring assistance to leper women, particularly the more abandoned.

Two or three times a year, religious fervor rose to a high

pitch and the parish experienced some hours of exaltation.

In 1874, hardly a year after his arrival, Father Damien organized a Corpus Christi procession. A Picpus Father who saw the ceremony left this description of it:

"Two repositories, decked with Hawaiian flags, had been erected; one at the tip of the peninsula, facing the sea; the other, on the grounds of the hospital. The canopy and a portable altar nine feet high were made of bamboo that the men had cut in the mountains. Instead of paint, they used red and white paper in spirals for decoration. Inasmuch as someone had recently made Father a gift of twenty new curtains for his chapel, he had given the old ones to the women to make albs and cinctures, oriflammes and large banners.

"At three o'clock, the procession was set in motion. It was arranged in three divisions. First, with three fringed banners with thirty oriflammes fluttering above them, walked the children, then the girls, then the adults. This first division was followed by the portable altar, carried at the head of the band, the women's choir and the men's choral group. Then came the Blessed Sacrament. Four strong men in green coats decorated with red crosses supported the canopy. At each of its four corners marched an acolyte in a cassock, carrying a torch. In front of the canopy, the choir boys in surplices were swinging censers. They themselves were preceded by little girls clothed in white and blue, who scattered flowers on the roadway. Another band of instrumentalists brought up the rear of the procession.

"Without a break, the recitation of the Rosary went on, while the band played and the choirs chanted each in its turn.

"Father Damien walked under the canopy, holding the ostensorium. He proceeded slowly; accommodating his pace to some cripples who were finding it hard to follow. Tears were rolling down his cheeks.

"The whole leprosarium was in attendance. Even non-Catholics raised their hats at the passing of the Blessed Sacrament. Many of them joined the procession, some even in the front ranks. On the following Sunday, eight of them came to ask for baptism."

Christmas, too, was a feast of special solemnity. We see the Noel of 1882 through a letter in journal form, which Damien addressed to Pamphile:

"December 22. This morning, after Mass, instructions and confessions. In the afternoon, I hear the confessions of the sick in the hospital who are unable to come to church. The nose and ears of the confessor are sorely tried on such occasions. I can stop up one of these organs, but leave the others open.

"December 23. Fast day. The salt I mix with my *poi* must take the place of customary good meat. At half past six, I take Holy Communion to the hospital, which is ten minutes from the church. Some of the sick are blind or have badly damaged lips and I must be very careful. A well educated non-Catholic received conditional absolution. After Mass, we begin to sweep and decorate the church. My young people have plaited long ropes of greenery which I nail to the arches of the altar. I put six candles into each of my wooden chandeliers.

"December 24. Sunday. I give the last touches to the altar. I am only half satisfied, having only old stuff at my disposal. The mice in the wardrobe have nibbled my altar frontal. At ten o'clock, High Mass, and after that my catechumens come seeking baptism without delay. Let us first have a bit of lunch. Meanwhile, my schoolmaster will examine the catechumens, and we shall see afterwards. I return at one o'clock: four Chinese and one Kanaka have been judged sufficiently prepared. These Chinese have had considerable difficulty in understanding the truths of our religion. I have instructed them through an interpreter, for I do not speak their tongue. Since they have been faithful in coming to Mass for six months, and since they are very sick, I decide to baptize them. The ceremony is over by two o'clock. Then I enter the confessional, where I remain until nine o'clock. Father Albert arrives afterwards with the Catholics from Kalaupapa.

"December 25. Christmas Day. At eleven p.m. (Christmas Eve) the bell rings a full peal. My young folks tour the village with their drums, waking everybody with the cry, 'Happy Christmas!' The weather is fine. The faithful hasten to arrive in their Sunday best. At 11:45 the bell rings again. We begin community prayers, then my singers break full-throated into the Christmas hymns. Precisely at midnight, Father Albert, preceded by acolytes, emerges from the sacristy and begins the ceremony. The brightly lighted church is crowded. There is perfect order. The sermon makes a deep impression. At about two o'clock all is over, and my beloved Kanakas return to their homes.

"This is the ninth Midnight Mass I have celebrated here. In the early years, some excesses occurred. But now my people are more civilized and everything goes well.

"At dawn, I celebrate my second Mass. Since I am permitted to do it, I ring the bell very loud. Everybody sleeps through it; nobody comes to Mass.

"At ten o'clock, High Mass, at which everybody assists. At five o'clock, benediction followed by catechism."

Instrumental and choral music enlivened all the feasts.

When Bishop Maigret came to confirm the lepers in 1875, he was amazed by the pomp of his reception: two horses were waiting for him at the landing; a Mozart Mass was rendered at the church; with band blaring, a procession of two hundred people headed by flags and drums escorted him back to his boat.

The band also performed at burials. There were several burials every week, since about one hundred and fifty persons died in the course of a year.

"I was in the church, reciting my office," recalled a missionary, "when distant sounds of music crept into my ears. As the procession gradually came nearer, I distinguished the boom of bass-drums, the roll of snare drums, the sounds of the wood-winds and the brasses.

"Soon the church filled up. Father Damien pronounced the absolution, then the procession started toward the cemetery.

"Some women held the ends of ribbons of the pall: others, in double file, followed the hearse. All were dressed in black and wore sashes, some red and some white, according to the confraternity to which they belonged. The men followed, in mourning clothes. The band brought up the rear. Never have I seen musicians take so much satisfaction in making music. Judging by the pieces they played, one could not doubt but that the dead woman whose corpse they were escorting to its final resting place was already in paradise.

"Father Damien had the same thought; for on returning from the cemetery, he remarked: 'Poor Juliana! She was so good. She is surely in heaven, for she passed through her purgatory here below.'

'Are your burials always like this one?'

'Always! Our Kanakas love pomp, and our confraternities consider it their duty to solemnize the funeral ceremonies.'"

Police Work

It would not do to conclude that all the lepers had become little saints given to unceasing prayers and good works. Although drunkenness and debauchery had notably diminished, they had not disappeared. Drunkards did have to go far out of their way for a drink.

As Father Damien's report of 1886 tells us, "There grows along the Pali a plant called *ki*, from the roots of which is made a very intoxicating liquor. At the time of my arrival, the lepers consumed huge quantities of it. Once drunk from it, they forgot even the most elementary restraints of decency. It is easier to imagine their actions than to describe them. The administration had to put an end to such abominations. The superintendent and

I made a tour of inspection, and either by persuasion or by threats we succeeded in getting possession of stills and other apparatus for making liquor."

To destroy the stills was not enough. To prevent the setting up of new stills, the police who had been hand in glove with the criminals had to be supplanted.

Some agents of the Board and some employees were also agents of debauchery. If they were not lepers, Damien could exercise little control over them; but he was quick to drive them out of the lazaretto.

He declared that, though he allowed for exceptions, the presence of non-sick, unmarried persons was not desirable.

On the other hand, he had promoted the idea that married couples not be parted when one of them had to come to the island: "My ministry has let me see at close quarters the sad consequences of separating man and wife. It favors license when it is not a torture for the exiled man or woman, as it frequently is. When the spouses remain together, they more easily grow resigned to their lot and give each other the affectionate care that outsiders cannot give."

If his advice had been followed, all employees of the lazaretto would have been chosen from among the healthy men.

"The others," continues the report, "are not at all suitable except in cases of long experience and tested loyalty. Some are selfish, well-paid men who give no service in return and waste their wages in gaming. Some are loafers who go from house to house sponging upon the slender rations of the sick and stealing their clothing. Some, finally, are debauched characters who induce some lepers to take part in their shameful acts."

His constant dread of a return to former corrupt practices gave Damien the courage to draw up an indictment, like the foregoing of some employees of the administration.

At long intervals, riots broke out. At times, too, there were attempts to raise once again the altars of the goddess *Laka* and to perform lascivious dances before them.

There were many non-Catholics at the leprosarium. In theory, these were outside the jurisdiction of Father Damien. But in theory only; for, in practice, he had enough moral authority and physical strength to stop any disorder on the part of anyone.

Some employees and some lepers, whose game he had spoiled, bore a grudge against him; but he kept them all in awe of him.

Rarely has police work been more effectively done. Evildoers trembled in his presence; and when he broke into their brawls and orgies, his huge stick in his hand, the culprits fled as fast as they could. Hutchinson, who saw him in action, assures us that no one dared resist him and that he succeeded in dispersing the most unruly mobs. "I have known only one other man at the leprosarium as resolute and as dreaded as Father Damien. This was a giant named Kekelaupio, who without batting an eyelash would shoulder a weight of eight hundred pounds, or flatten the huskiest scamp just with the back of his hand. He made his presence felt while he was there. But, when all is said, it was especially to Father Damien that the reign of law and order was due."

What a transformation he brought about!

Stoddard, who had visited the leprosarium in 1868 and returned in 1884, could not believe his eyes. Instead of a cattle-run, a convict prison, a place where evil reigned, a settlement of dirty hovels into which lepers were thrown to rot and die as in a roadside ditch, he now saw flower gardens, fields under cultivation, a hospital in which the more serious cases were properly nursed, two cemeteries where the dead were reverently buried, and orphanages filled with happy children. He met men and women on horseback on the way to join a procession. Bells rang in belfries, and churches were crowded with the faithful. Feast days gave a welcome opportunity for all kinds of public rejoicing. There were work and prayer and relaxation in proper proportion. Sorrow found consolation, since the sick had daily visits from their Father and when their hour came, gave up their spirit in his arms. In a word, the life of the community flowed along almost as normally and as smoothly as life anywhere else.

"Aren't you homesick?" a visitor once asked lepers he met here and there along the road.

They replied in effect: "Oh, no! We are well off here. The government watches over us, our superintendent is very kind and we are particularly happy over our pastor. He builds our houses with his own hands; he gives us tea, biscuits, sugar and clothing; he takes care of us, not letting us lack for anything. We wouldn't want to lose all this by leaving our beloved *Makua Kamiano*."

Clifford wrote: "I had been told that this place was a hell. But now I ask myself whether there are not some compensations here that are unknown in other parts of the globe. In very truth, these poor people seem to be singularly happy."

Damien, too, was content and wrote to his aged mother: "I am very happy with my lepers and for nothing in this world would I wish to be separated from them."

Chapter 11

World Fame and Hawaiian Honors

Like all others who take an active part in the drama of life, Damien had his friends and his enemies. Fortunately, the friends were so numerous and so loyal that the enemies were unable to do any lasting harm to his work.

Money—much money—was required for his work. His friends saw to it that he received it.

Scarcely had Damien settled down at Molokai when "twelve persons at a chance meeting in Honolulu, contributed the sum of fifty francs each" to be sent to him. Among those twelve benefactors of his early days were ten non-Catholics. Although not always in this same proportion, Protestants and other non-Catholics never ceased exercising a magnificent generosity in behalf of his work.

Two months after landing at the leprosarium, Damien sailed to Honolulu, where he went begging from door to door; and he returned to Molokai with apparel to clothe more than three hundred of the lepers.

His brothers in religion gave him assistance according to their means. His Mission, which had under its care all the posts in the Archipelago, did what it could for him according to circumstance – now allotments of money, now suggestions for economizing. From Paris, the procurator general cooperated, too, either by drawing on the funds of the congregation or by transmitting alms he had received.

Among the most steady collaborators of Father Damien were the Picpus Sisters in Honolulu, who added to their religious zeal a feminine adroitness in getting everybody they met interested in his cause. From their convent an unfailing stream of financial gifts and bundles of clothing was directed toward the leprosarium.

Help from Abroad

The most magnificent of all Damien's benefactors, however, were his English and American friends.

Father Damien and his cause early won favorable attention in England and, indeed, never lost their popularity in that kingdom.

In the London suburb of Camberwell at that time lived an Anglican priest, the pastor of St. Luke's Church and a gentleman of generous instincts, the Reverend Hugh B. Chapman. After having chanced to read an article dealing with Molokai, he spoke about Damien from his pulpit and invited his parishioners to be generous in helping him. In order to widen his appeal by permitting Catholics within his parish boundaries to combine their mites with the contributions of the Anglicans, Reverend Chapman sought and obtained for his campaign the approval of Cardinal Manning, Catholic Archbishop of Westminster.

The Reverend Mr. Chapman received 675 pounds sterling (about three thousand three hundred dollars), a notable sum from a poor, nineteenth-century Anglican parish giving alms for a Catholic priest. He thanked the donors through the following circular printed in the London *Tablet*:

I wish to inform you that, having gathered 650 pounds, we shall close our first subscription list next Saturday. I voice my respectful thanks to you for having contributed in this way to the little offering that I shall be happy to send to the holy priest of Molokai. Any discussion with reference to the sublime charity that he practices would be simply an impertinence. His life makes ours look very selfish and slack, and it is a great honor for us to place our homage at the feet of such a man. As for those who have any objection, whatever it may be, they are much more to be pitied than he.

Your humble servant,

H.B. Chapman

117, Camden Grove, North Peckham

November 10, 1886

Americans, to whom Hawaii and things Hawaiian were no longer foreign, imitated the generosity of the English. American writers and doctors paid many visits to Molokai.

Dr. G.W. Woods, director of the Brooklyn Hospital, landed there in 1876:

"Quite a squadron of lepers on horseback came to meet me," he wrote. "They were headed by the under-superintendent, Ragsdale (himself a leper) and by Father Damien. The latter was then the picture of health. He had a fine head covered with rumpled black hair and a smiling, gentle face.

"'This is my work here,' he said while conducting me around the lazaretto. 'Sooner or later, I shall become a leper, but I ask God that it may not happen before I have come to the end of my ability to help these poor children!'"

In 1883 Damien said to Dr. Kueln, another American physician: "Personally, I have no needs. But if you wish to give me pleasure, send me again some clothes to outfit my lepers."

He thought only of his lepers. As for himself, at that very moment he was so impoverished that he did not have pennies enough even to pay the postage on his correspondence.

After his second visit to the lazaretto, C. W. Stoddard wrote:

"Other lepers gathered about us as we entered the churchyard...and as their number increased, it seemed as if each newcomer was more horrible than the last, until corruption could go no farther and flesh suffer no deeper dishonor this side of the grave. They voluntarily drew aside as we advanced....

"The chapel door stood ajar; in a moment it was thrown open and a young priest paused on the threshold to give us welcome."

The publication of reports like the foregoing raised up for Damien many benefactors in America. From every corner of this country, bundles and checks were sent to him. A Boston pastor sent him a very fine harmonium. Bankers in Portland advanced him funds without requiring any interest. This generous gesture had been inspired by Archbishop Groos of Portland, Oregon, who assumed the title of "American business agent for the lepers." In this capacity, he shared honors with the Rev. Mr. Chapman of England.

The humble priest on Molokai had become, so to speak, an international star. His praises were sung even in the German press. A Protestant who had returned from Oceania printed the following in a Berlin newspaper:

"A Catholic priest has gone to that hell of the lepers. He is the only one who has had the courage to enter there and to remain there in order to give those abandoned souls the consolations of eternal life. Travelers from every country, pause and salute as you pass the rocks of Molokai!"

Such fame was a priceless aid to the priest. It not only sent material assistance rolling toward him: it also served to protect him against the pursuit of his enemies. The admiration he enjoyed in every quarter preserved him from becoming a victim of misunderstanding and jealousy. As a matter of fact, the only thing that prevented his expulsion from the midst of his lepers was the certainty that noble minds throughout the world would have been quick to denounce such cruelty.

Among the friends who were in the forefront of Damien's defense, it is but fair to name his superior general, Father Sylvan Bousquet. The ridiculous reports that the general received did not in the least shake his confidence in his subordinate. He understood his great-souled spiritual son, and in spite of all remonstrances he kept him at his post.

Nor should we fail to note the admirable Bishop Maigret, who was his bishop up to 1881; nor good Father Modeste, who was Damien's provincial until 1878.

Royal Recognition

If we seem to pass over the names of Mr. Meyer and other champions, it is because we have noted their loyalty in preceding pages. It remains to mention Mr. Walter Gibson, long-time president of the Board of Health and, for a while, premier of Hawaii; and, finally, several members of the royal family, particularly the princesses Liliuokalani and Kapiolani.

King Kalakaua was at that time engaged in his travels around the world. His sister, Princess Liliuokalani, who was acting as regent, took advantage of her temporary rank to arrange a royal visit to the lepers and a royal decoration for their pastor.

On September 15, 1881, the queen (she bore that title in the absence of the king) took passage on the steamer *Lekua*. She was attended by her sister, Princess Likelike; the premier, Honorable Kapena; ladies of honor; and army officers.

When the steamer had dropped anchor before Kalaupapa, flower-decked boats brought the passengers to the landing-place, which a temporary wharf, garlanded with flowers, had transformed and beautified. Seven hundred lepers thronged the beach. A little farther inland, a pavilion resembling a Kanaka cabin had been erected with a flower-strewn pathway leading to its entrance. Escorted by sixty-six lepers in sketchy uniforms of more or less military design, the queen passed under several triumphal arches on her way to this pavilion.

Amid sustained applause, she took her place on the dais, surrounded by her escort. A leper choir of young girls clothed in white and wearing sashes of rose and blue advanced to sing a lengthy native chant. Some of the girls concealed their hands; others stood sideways to keep from the royal sight the sores that disfigured them; still others held handkerchiefs before their mouths. The queen listened to their singing; but she could not refrain from giving closer attention to their appearance.

On recognizing some friends in the pathetic audience, the princess burst into tears. Members of the royal suite did not find it difficult to follow this example. The singing ended in choking sobs. The queen got up to speak, but tears strangled her, and her words stuck in her throat. The premier, the Honorable Kapena, stepped forward and saved the day by giving a speech that touched the hearts of all.

With Father Damien and Mr. Meyer as guides, the royal party then set out on a tour of the leprosarium. The queen insisted on seeing everything: dwellings, hospital, orphanages, churches, priest-house, stores. Her sensitive woman's mind understood the nature of Father Damien's achievements and she paid him the warmest compliments.

However, the sadness that had chilled her soul on the dais stayed with her throughout the day. She took away a sorely wounded heart.

There were some distressing scenes at the place of embarkation that evening. The queen had been accompanied by relatives of the afflicted, who now had to tear themselves away from the wife, the husband, the children they had found again for a day. One mother hugged her ten-year-old boy, his head swathed in bandages. Finally, it was necessary to use force to separate them and to carry her bodily to the steamer. For a long time, from the stern of the ship where she had collapsed on the deck, she kept her eyes fastened on her son who, perched on a rock, kept blowing kisses to her as long as she was within sight.

In the reports they published about the royal visit, the newspapers were high in their praise of Father Damien. "This young priest is the glory of Hawaii," sang one of them. "His heroism is greater than that of the Roman martyrs! Who would not consider it a godsend to be thrown to the wild animals in the arena rather than to be obliged to live in the poisoned air of a leprosarium?"

Since Damien was the "glory of Hawaii," it was eminently fitting that he be decorated. Liliuokalani saw to that without delay. Probably the good queen never had a happier moment than when she put her royal signature to this proclamation:

> Kalakaua, King of the Hawaiian Islands, To all who shall see these presents, greetings! We proclaim that we have appointed and by these presents, we do appoint
>
> Reverend Father Damien de Veuster
>
> *Knight Commander of our Royal Order of Kalakaua.*
>
> We give him title to exercise and to enjoy all the rights, perquisites and privileges which, by law, pertain to this Order, and to wear such insignia as established by warrant. In witness whereof we have issued these letters patent, and we have caused to be affixed thereon the seal of our Realm.
>
> Given under our hand in our palace at Honolulu this twenty-seventh day of September in the year of Our Lord eighteen hundred eighty-one.
>
> Liliuokalani, *Regent*

A letter from the queen informed Father Damien that he would be henceforward Knight Commander of the Order of Kalakaua:

> Reverend Sir, I desire to manifest my unalloyed admiration for the heroic and unselfish services that you are rendering to the most unhappy people of this kingdom and to convey in some measure the homage of the populace for the devotion, the patience and the limitless charity with which you work for the corporal and spiritual relief of all those unfortunate persons unavoidably deprived of the affectionate care of their relatives and of their friends.
>
> I know very well that your labors and sacrifices have no other motive than the desire to do good to those in distress; and that you look for no reward except from the great God, our Sovereign Lord, who directs and inspires you. Nevertheless, to content my earnest desire, I beg of you, Reverend Father, to accept the decoration of Knight Commander of the Royal Order of Kalakaua, as a testimony of my sincere admiration for the efforts you are making to relieve the distress and lessen the sufferings of these afflicted people, as I myself had occasion to see on my recent visit to the settlement.
>
> Your friend,
> Liliuokalani, Regent

Nothing in the world could leave Damien more indifferent than a decoration. He took it rather lightheartedly. After listing for Pamphile the labors which were wearing him down, he wrote: "In addition, from two o'clock to nine o'clock, Sir Knight will have to remain in the confessional." Seriously speaking, he was ready to become commander and knight of all the orders in the world, if doing so would serve the cause of his lepers.

Damien replied to Queen Liliuokalani in accordance with protocol, informing her that he accepted, "however unworthy," from her royal hands "the honorable title of Knight Commander of the Order Of Kalakaua, as a token of the concord and mutual respect that exist between the royal family and the Catholic Church."

He concluded with this expression, which he could not have written without a smile:

"Touching my mission at Kalawao, I give my word as Knight Commander of the Order of Kalakaua that I will devote all my energy to the spiritual and bodily welfare of the unfortunate lepers."

The official conferring of the decoration on the new dignitary and the celebration of this event with appropriate ceremony were still on the calendar.

Aging Bishop Maigret was about to retire from his bishopric, and a coadjutor, Bishop Kockeman, had just been sent to him. The queen assigned to this new bishop the distinction of conferring the badge of honor. He has left an account of his trip to Molokai and his experiences there:

"When we landed at Kaunakakai in the southern part of the island at 2:00 a.m., we caught sight of Father Damien, who was waiting for us in the moonlight. He brought us to the former country villa of King Kamehameha V, where we took a little rest. At dawn, we mounted our horses and after two hours' ride across an arid countryside, we arrived at the home of Mr. Meyer, who, with his family, welcomed us and invited us to breakfast.

"Toward half-past ten, we reached the summit of the gigantic mountains which overhang the leprosarium. Now was the time for the strenuous descent of the notorious Pali. We turned our horses and a mule over to a servant of Mr. Meyer; then, with our luggage on our backs, we began the descent at noon. That dangerous and fatiguing descent lasted an hour and a quarter. It was necessary to cling to tree trunks and to rocks, to slide on one's back and to skirt with care the chasm into which a whole herd of steers had stumbled to perish some weeks before. Even now, the stench of their rotting carcasses assailed our nostrils. Seeing me wilting under the weight of my luggage, Father Damien, who is as strong as a Turk, shouldered the load himself.

"....We were welcomed at the foot of the mountain by the band and a squadron of sixty-six horsemen, each carrying a pennon; they escorted us with music to Kalawao, a mile and a quarter away."

The bishop spoke at length of the civil and religious ceremonies that marked that memorable day. One can easily picture the garlands of flowers, the cavalcades, the shouts of joy from crowds where Catholics and non-Catholics rubbed shoulders, the reading of Liliuokalani's letter and of the citation, and finally the solemn moment when, amid wild outbursts of enthusiastic cheers, the insignia of the Order of Kalakaua was pinned on the breast of Father Damien.

The Honolulu newspapers once again blew the jubilant trumpets to celebrate the glory of the Father of the lepers:

"We are so much the more pleased over what has just occurred," said the *Commercial Advertiser*, "for the reason that the queen has not hesitated to rise above the squabbling of certain small cliques, to deal justly with the merits of a Catholic priest. May that consecrated man remain always among us, and for a long time to come may he take pleasure from the honors he has so justly achieved."

These well deserved honors did not succeed in turning Father Damien's head. On the very day on which the distinction was bestowed, the bishop had to be asked to order him to keep the medallion pinned on his breast until the evening. When Clifford arrived later and expressed astonishment at not finding it displayed, Damien replied wryly: "It would humiliate my old patched cassock!" However, on national holidays, he used to wear his ribbon as a sign of his loyalty to the Hawaiian authorities, or as a concession to his lepers, to whom the trinket seemed to give so much pleasure. "To genuine worth," wrote Father Jourdan, "the apostle joined the humility that was his crowning virtue." Without doubt. But this particular act of virtue did not cost him much.

The days were coming, however, when his humility would meet severe trials.

"The prejudice, the spite and the mean spirit of certain cliques," to use the language of the *Commercial Advertiser*, came to life again to his heavy cost. Piqued by the conferring of Damien's knighthood, persecution was on the march again.

And, in addition, he was about to become a leper!

Part Three

Damien the Leper

Chapter 12

Stricken

It is not known just when the disease from which he was to die began to attack Damien. Because its onset is gradual, Hansen's disease is difficult to detect in its early stages.

Perhaps we should look back to his days at Kohala. Even at that time, he had observed that contact with the lepers among his parishioners left him with "a sort of itching or burning" on his face and legs.

During his first years on Molokai, the same phenomenon occurred with greater frequency and intensity. In a reminiscent mood in later days, Damien expressed the opinion that the disease was already in him early in his apostolate on Molokai.

Indications of Infection

In 1874, for example, he felt a dull pain in his feet. The burning sensation in them made him feverish and restless and drove away sleep until he began to soak his feet in cold water and leave them uncovered throughout the night.

At some point in 1876, his arms and back became covered

with dry, yellowish spots. It is interesting to hear that these spots became less troublesome when Father drank sarsaparilla and returned in force when he stopped drinking it.

By June, 1878, Damien's superiors no longer hesitated to express their judgment that he had become a victim of leprosy. "The leprosarium is entrusted to the loving care of Father Damien, himself a leper," wrote Father Modeste in a letter to the superior general.

Yet, in January, 1879, Damien regarded himself as completely cured. "My health is very good," he wrote to the general. "All the unpleasant symptoms have disappeared."

Fifteen months later, however, he must have had a disquieting relapse, for on April 6, 1880, the vice-provincial, Father Regis, was happy to inform his superior in Paris: "Reassuring news: Father Damien is not leprous. In the judgment of a wise physician experienced in this field, his illness was only an infection of the bloodstream. It has disappeared."

That diagnosis was later shown to be far from accurate. In the autumn of 1881 violent pains invaded Damien's left foot. During the ensuing year, they advanced through the leg. In particular, the inflamed sciatic nerve tortured the priest up until June, 1885. In the meantime, an area of insensibility developed and spread over one side of his left foot.

Certitude

To remove all uncertainty about his infection, Damien made an experiment. He plunged his feet into water which he knew to be boiling hot. He felt no pain, but upon withdrawing them, he saw large blisters form and ribbons of skin fall away.

There could be no further doubt. He had leprosy!

When the celebrated Dr. Arning was passing through Molokai, Damien sought his advice. With the aid of a microscope and other devices then in use, the physician discovered the presence of Hansen's bacillus in the suspect tissues. Although at first he hesitated to make his diagnosis known, he was persuaded to do so by the priest's fortitude: "What you have supposed is true. In your turn, you have been stricken."

"My mind has always been prepared for that," replied Damien. "As a matter of fact, for a long time I have been certain of having leprosy."

The progress of the disease now became rapid. Tubercles appeared on his left ear, which became inordinately large. His eyebrows fell out. His powerful hands and his handsome face became covered with swellings and sores.

"Soon I shall be completely disfigured," he wrote to his bishop. "But I stay calm, resigned and quite happy in the midst of my people."

To his new provincial, Father "L," he wrote: "There is no longer any doubt about my trouble: I am a leper. Blessed be God! Do not pity me too much. I ask but one favor: send me in this tomb someone who can be my confessor."

In truth, he might as well have been walled up in a tomb. No one had come to take Father Albert's place, and a strict ordinance prevented any leper from leaving the island even for a few hours.

Damien did not give much thought to the prospect of an early death. He even made efforts to cheer others up in the face of his affliction:

"My very Reverend Father," he wrote to his general, "do not be too sad because one of your sons has been decorated, not only with the Royal Cross of Kalakaua, but also with the heavier and less honorable cross of leprosy. It is the inevitable consequence of my being here. My robust constitution long resisted the invasion, but has finally been undermined by the infiltration of the bacilli into my members. However, I am still on my feet, and, by exercising prudence, I hope to continue my work as heretofore."

The news rapidly ran across two continents and shocked his friends into redoubling their affection and their generosity toward him. It also distressed his enemies, to whom his renown had always been a thorn in the side. Some took the opportunity to give a dig: his illness, they said, was the result of his imprudence and lack of personal care.

They were partly right: Father Damien had committed the initial imprudence of going to Molokai and had compounded this serious imprudence by remaining there.

As for his deficiencies in the matter of personal care, under pressure of unending work the priest may have relaxed some of the precautions he had at first laid down for himself. In the beginning, he had forbidden lepers to enter the priest-house, and he had shown great respect for cleanliness. But out of fear of offending his lepers by appearing to be over-cautious and fastidious, he had become bolder in his contacts with the afflicted. It was possible, too, that he had grown a little skeptical about his ultimate chances of escaping contagion.

In his report of 1886, he expressed his opinion that "leprosy is contracted by inoculation and respiration."

How, then, could there be protection from contagion for this priest, who in his daily work among the lepers heard their confessions, administered the last sacraments to them, lived with them and labored by their side? He inhaled their fetid breath, touched their sores and handled their tools as they handled his. It was not seldom that he cut himself, or scraped his skin, or bruised his hand when he sawed, planed, squared or nailed, for his avocation of carpenter and builder required him to squeeze manual labor into his crowded daily schedule.

"He was in the habit of smoking," an eyewitness reported, "and from time to time he laid his pipe on his workbench. The lepers who were working with him, or the children who usually surrounded him, profited from this opportunity to take a puff or two." Could he have succeeded in keeping them from doing this by pleading that they might infect him?

To his brother Pamphile, who was sick at the time, he broke the news in cautious terms: "I have been greatly distressed to hear of your illness. You tell me that you seem to be declining into consumption. God grant that it be not so. As for me, I can no longer hide from you the fact that I am threatened with a still more terrible disease. Leprosy, you know, is contagious. In point of fact, I am as robust as you have always known me to be. But for three years my left foot has been losing all ability to feel anything. I have in my body a poison, as it were, that threatens to taint the whole organism. Let us not talk too loud and let us pray for each other."

Letters to His Mother

In writing to his aged mother, he confined himself to saying that it was only a little "inflammation."

His letter was in French:

> Beloved Mother,
>
> Forgive me for not writing in Flemish. I have not forgotten our beautiful mother-tongue, but the words no longer come easily to me and that is the reason, too, that I have failed to send you news for such a long time.

The preceding year, he had had to labor at writing a rough draft of a letter in Flemish before copying it over to send.

> Pardon me for writing so seldom. As the years go by, I find myself more and more absorbed by the duties of my ministry and by the care of the sick. Thanks be to God, my health is fairly good. I stay about the same, except for my beard, which is now about an inch thick and is touched with white.
>
> I am always in the midst of from seven to eight

hundred lepers. I have already filled one cemetery with the dead. Soon, for want of needed space, we shall have to dig deeper and lay the coffins one on top of the other....

For two months now, I have not been too well. It happened this way: I was returning to the lazaretto in a small boat, but could not land because of the high sea. The captain set me down on a rock not far from the beach and I had to reach the shore by swimming. I arrived home soaked to the skin, and since then I have had a heavy cold.

Let me tell you about another accident. When I was taking a footbath recently, I was careless enough to put my feet into water that was almost at the boiling point. At the time, the skin fell away from the flesh; but it has renewed itself already. The inflammation has begun to diminish, and soon I shall be completely whole again. While I am convalescing, I have a little difficulty in saying Mass. I have to sit down while preaching, and since I am unable to walk, I get around in a carriage. Thus, in the midst of my sick people, I play at being sick myself....

A doctor has strongly recommended that I go home and breathe my native air for a while. But what would become of my wretched children here? No. Since I have so much opportunity for doing a little good here, I will remain at my post until I die. We shall never see each other again here below, but we shall in heaven, where there will be no separation—ever.

Madame de Veuster had been a widow for thirteen years. She was now in her eighty-third year and her health was failing. At first the family succeeded in concealing the shocking fact from her. But it was in the newspapers, and soon a tattling woman broke the news. Madame de Veuster wept a long time, then said, "Well, I shall go to heaven with him."

She was no longer able to read, but she managed to have someone read her the reports in the newspapers. Had not one of them said that "the flesh of the leper priest of Molokai fell away from his bones in strips?" This priest that the papers pictured as disfigured and rotting was flesh of her flesh, her handsome boy, so courageous, so affectionate, so dear to her. She had carefully preserved in a drawer, like a treasure, his last letters to her. Now her imagination placed him on a rock in the middle of the ocean, deserted, dying of slow torture far from her arms, without a kiss, without a soothing word, without help of any kind.

Her old heart could not long survive the shock. She yielded her grasp on life and set about preparing for her journey to the rendezvous in heaven that her son had arranged.

On the morning of April 6, 1886, she felt that she was about to die and begged not to be left alone. She kept murmuring prayers and repeating the aspirations that were whispered in her ear. Toward 4:00 p.m., she turned her eyes for the last time toward the portrait of her Joseph hanging on the wall and then, tilting her head to the side, breathed a last gentle sigh.

Dutton – a lay volunteer who came from the U.S. to work with Father Damien in his last years – was with the priest when he received the sad news of his mother's death. "Joseph," Damien said simply, "pray for my good old mother."

"His grief was not effusive," added Dutton. "He believed that, after a lifetime of duty well done, his mother had gone to heaven." And he knew that it would not be long before he joined her.

Father Damien after his arrival on Molokai, 1873

Damien the leper, Winter, 1889

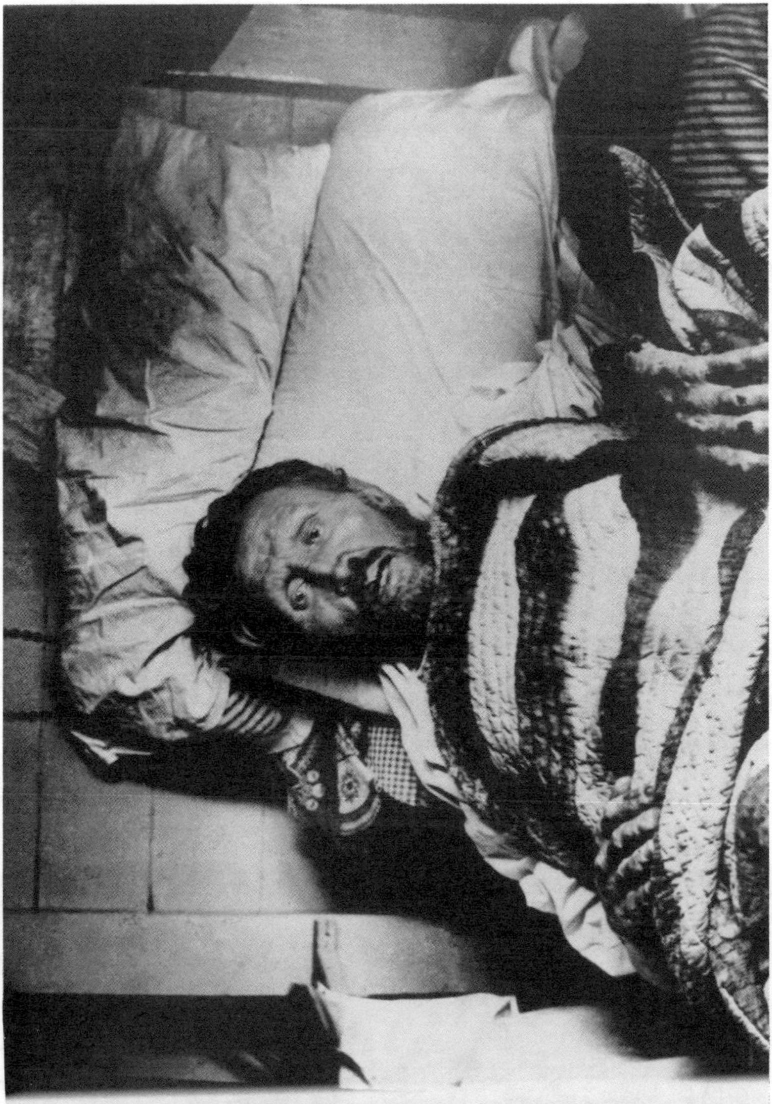

Father Damien on his deathbed, April, 1889

Grave monument to Father Damien, Molokai

Chapter 13

Final Labors

Far from quenching Damien's zeal, the disease seemed to inflame it more intensely. His time for quitting this world was in sight, and that prospect seemed to drive him toward the full accomplishment of all his plans for the welfare of the lepers.

Now that he could walk only with difficulty, he rode on horseback or drove about in a carriage drawn by his old nag, William.

"My looks are not what they used to be," he wrote, "but the leprosy has not yet attacked my hands." He therefore continued to work with his hands quite as effectively as he had in the past.

Father Damien had become for all practical purposes the director of the leprosarium. Under the administration of Mr. Gibson and (after June, 1887) of Mr. Trousseau, the Board generally followed his suggestions.

The Report

In January, 1886, he was urged to embody in a report the lessons he had learned through his long experience. At first he shrank from the fatigue that such an effort would require. "I am sick and I am bowed down by my work," he wrote to the secretary of the general, "and I strain my eyesight in writing even the most necessary letters and in reading my breviary at night." Nevertheless, he did what he could: "For the honor of the Mission, I devoted to the task all my little talent."

That report was a document of fifty pages written in English and covering of the following eight topics:

The advantages of a good diet;

The need for potable water;

The advantages of proper housing;

The need for decent and warm clothing;

The usefulness of physical exercise;

The fairness of permitting married couples to continue their home life;

The wholesomeness of morality and the foulness of debauchery;

The judicious use of medications.

To the report was added an appendix which dealt with the spread of Hansen's disease. The author noted that before contracting Hansen's disease, nine-tenths of his sick had shown symptoms of syphilis. As for the remainder: "I attest that they became lepers without being syphilitic. Their disease is due to contagion, either through inhalation or through inoculation."

This report was marked by prudence, humility and charity. It did not violate good taste. The author was an honest man who told the truth without glossing over or exaggerating. He had the mental balance to proceed in orderly fashion, to attempt only the feasible and to give proof of his assertions. He also had the heart of a hero who minimized his own efforts but could not hide his readiness to sacrifice his life a hundred times if thereby he could keep the lepers from ever again being treated as the scum of society.

The Board of Health implemented the recommendations

set down in Damien's report. With the eyes of the whole world now upon Molokai, the Hawaiian government was more than ever inclined to do its duty toward its lepers.

In the final accounting, Damien was to succeed in winning for his "children" almost everything he had set out to achieve.

New Projects

In 1887, the Board sent him the materials for building two wooden dormitories for his orphans. "They are," he said, "the largest and the neatest in all the leprosarium." In each of them a hundred children could be sheltered. A little later, he built some dining halls in the same proportions.

His lepers at Kalawao had plenty of good drinking water, drawn from the reservoir through a conduit previously constructed by the priest. At Kalaupapa, however, they had none at all, but had to go and fetch their water from a place three miles away. In 1886, Father Damien discovered two springs with a flow sufficient to supply the whole leprosarium. One was at Paihamau, the other at Wailuku. He made studies, he drew up plans, he gave hints, he wrote entreaties. The Board voted a credit of $35,000. On May 6, 1887, Mr. Meyer announced that the construction work would soon begin. "The water will come from Wailuku and thus no one will ever again lack water. In the near future, the pipes will arrive from San Francisco. I have already ordered six yoke of oxen for hauling them to the places where they will be used." When all was ready, Damien put his able-bodied men to work on the project and in a short time it was completed.

Meanwhile, a new treatment for Hansen's disease had been introduced at the hospital at Kakaako near Honolulu. It was the discovery of a Japanese physician, Dr. Goto. This regimen promised to be more efficacious than the pills of *Hoang-Nan* had been. As a matter of fact, it did relieve the disease, but it did not cure it. Damien studied the method with great care.

"It consists," he wrote, "in taking every day two hot baths in water into which certain solution has been poured; and in swallowing at each meal, a gram of certain pills and, one hour later, an ounce of a certain infusion. The Board supplied me with a bathtub and a bath heater. I have tried this procedure for several weeks with fifty of my children and we all feel greatly benefited as a result." Appetite and sleep returned and pains ceased.

In order to have all his lepers take advantage of this treatment, Damien put before the Board his plans for a center where one hundred lepers could take the cure. It was all envisioned in detail: a room for steam boilers; fifteen bathtubs; two bath halls eleven yards by three, a dining hall twenty yards by six; a kitchen seven yards by five; six dormitories thirteen yards by six; not to mention another large bath hall to be used by lepers coming from a distance. All these structures were to be erected within an enclosure 130 yards by 110, to be laid out to the east of his priest-house.

On August 10, 1886, Mr. Gibson wrote that he would be happy to assist Damien in his project. He added that a large consignment of Japanese medicine had just arrived. But four months later, on December 6, he had to notify the priest that when the Board had realized the cost of putting Damien's plan into effect, it had recoiled from the expense. But Gibson added: "If you find it possible to renovate already existing buildings, we are prepared to assist you."

It goes without saying that Father Damien managed to make his "existing buildings" serve his purpose. He turned one of them "into a fine bath hall," where he himself and a hundred other lepers followed the Goto regimen.

In Damien's final days on Molokai, there was an echo of his first. Before his hands had become completely useless, he built his last church.

He had long contemplated replacing Brother Bertrand's

chapel with a more permanent church, and that year a hurricane had blown down the belfry of St. Philomena's. Not long afterward, two beautiful tabernacles came as gifts from America—one for Kalawao, the other for Kalaupapa. Certainly, each would have to be placed in a fitting setting.

"We have just set the tabernacle at Kalawao on a stonework base three feet square," Damien wrote to one of his benefactors. "On account of its weight, we had to exercise considerable care in placing it there, for our tools were quite inadequate. The retable rises almost to the ceiling. If I succeed in building for this tabernacle the altar it deserves, we shall have a truly magnificent ensemble. Our lepers stand before it in admiration, marveling at the perfection of detail achieved by your American artisans. Since this altar will cover more floor space than its predecessor, and since the number of my faithful is steadily growing, it will be necessary to find some way of enlarging the church. Fortunately, my hands, though covered with sores, can still be used in such a work."

The Americans had furnished the tabernacle; the English would have to be invited to build the church to house it fittingly.

Damien did not consider it proper to ask Dr. Chapman in London to interest his coreligionists in a project so unequivocally Catholic. He simply asked him to pass on the word about it to Cardinal Manning.

The cardinal responded by sending his special blessing, but it was left to Dr. Chapman to raise the required funds. The contributions of English Protestants bulked large in the total collection. The pastor of St. Luke's in London made a point of reassuring Damien about the intentions of his coreligionists. "This money," he wrote to the priest, "is intended for the erection of a chapel for your *Catholic* lepers, and you are to use it as you wish. All the contributors are only too happy to give this evidence of their respectful affection."

So rapidly was this church erected around its tabernacle

that Father Jourdan wondered whether the Angels had not conspired to help Father Damien in building it.

As Damien planned it, the church was to be made of stone, in Gothic style, with a square tower surmounted by a balustrade and a metal roof. Only one skilled artisan was at hand to do the mason work, and he was a leper—as were those who dug up the stones, carted them, mixed the mortar and helped the priest with his carpentry.

A mishap occurred when they were transferring the metal roofplates, newly arrived from England, from the steamer to a skiff. The skiff capsized, and the full consignment of metal plates was dumped into the sea. For his iron roof, then, Father Damien had to substitute a makeshift covering. One of his confreres came unexpectedly upon him while he was engaged in this work.

"My amazed eyes caught sight of him up on his new church directing the roofing of it, giving orders to his masons, to his laborers, to his carpenters. With his swollen face, his enlarged ears, his reddened eyes and his muffled voice, he bore all the signs of being a genuine leper. But he worked as though he were in the pink of health and would be stopped only by the hand of death."

It was indeed his last building. Just a short time before his death, he put the final touches to it. The church still stands on Molokai.

Dutton, Damien's assistant in his last years, has written: "Realizing that his end was not far off, and seeing so many works still unfinished, Father summoned up all his strength to bring his projects into being. There can be little doubt that the extraordinary efforts of his final months whipped up the ravages of his leprosy and hastened the fatal outcome."

Nor did Damien relax in the performance of a single duty of his priestly vocation. The following letter indicates what Christmas entailed for him in 1886: "On the vigil, at five o'clock in the morning, I take my therapeutic bath. At six o'clock, I set out for Kalaupapa. I say Mass and preach, then I hear confessions until half-past eleven, all without breaking my fast. I return to Kalawao, where I take breakfast, then I enter the confessional, where I stay until seven o'clock. I recite my office. I drink a cup of coffee. At nine o'clock, I return to the church, where the children and the young people are waiting for a general examination in catechism which lasts until half-past eleven. At midnight begins the High Mass, at which I preach a half-hour sermon. At four o'clock in the morning, I am on my way back to Kalaupapa to sing my second Mass there and preach another sermon in the course of it. After Mass, I administer solemn baptism to some catechumens. At nine o'clock, I celebrate my third Mass, at Kalawao. By now I have reached the limit of my strength, and when the time comes for the sermon, one of my efficient catechists has to substitute for me. After all this, I must give some thought to preparing my Christmas dinner."

Chapter 14

Friends

In 1876, Damien had felt that everybody at the lazaretto held him in high esteem.

Later on, in proportion to his efforts to put down rebellions and stamp out orgies, he raised up enemies who came to look upon him as a police agent rather than as a man and a priest. But "those malefactors and blackguards" – to use the vigorous language of the leper Hutchinson – formed only a small clique.

This hostile faction lost most of its venom when the priest himself became a victim of Hansen's disease. Animosity dried up. Even his non-Catholic adversaries became reconciled, offering their friendly services to the afflicted man. The only exceptions were a former clergyman and some dissolute individuals who continued to slander the priest from afar off. We shall see how the mud they flung in his direction was later carefully shoveled up and put to use.

The news of his illness, deepened even more the affection of his friends, and drew several collaborators to his side.

Foremost among those whose friendship brought Damien great consolation were two English Protestants – an Anglican and a Calvinist – Chapman and Clifford; two American Catholic laymen, Dutton and Sinnet; and, finally, a Walloon priest without peer, Abbé Lambert Conrardy.

Rev. Hugh B. Chapman

To understand the noble mind and the generous heart of Rev. Hugh B. Chapman, it suffices to read some of his letters:

February 24, 1886

Reverend Father in Jesus Christ,

I write you in all humility to offer my deep and respectful sympathy to you whom a terrible disease has nailed to the cross.

If money can bring a measure of relief to those under your care, I shall undertake at once the collection of five hundred pounds to be sent to you.

I am of course, a minister of the Anglican Church, but your example is a sermon more helpful to your Church (and you) than the most beautiful discourse could be; and God is pleased to use it to lead me farther along the road of sacrifice to which Father Lacordaire has introduced me. I kneel before you and beg you to pray for me. I place the same great confidence in your prayers that I do in the prayers of my mother. Every day I ask God to put a speedy end to your suffering and to give you the crown you richly deserve. In eternity, I shall find myself too far away from you to see you; but from my outer place in the sanctuary I shall rejoice in your blessedness.

Please accept this letter as a slight token of my affection for you who have shown me what heroism means.

Hugh B. Chapman

Damien sent a reply on August 26:

Dear and Reverend Sir,

I bless our Lord for having given you, through the example of a poor priest who is merely doing his duty, an understanding of the sweetness of sacrifice. It is the Blessed Sacrament that teaches us how to renounce all human ambition. Without it, I might not have persevered in my resolve to share the lot of the lepers. Now that the expected has come to pass, the effects of leprosy begin to appear on my body. But Holy Communion makes me feel very happy in the somewhat unusual situation in which God has placed me....

I have with me a former member of the Episcopal Church of America who has become a Catholic. As a kind and sympathetic brother, without any remuneration, he assists me in the care of the lepers. He, too, finds his consolation in the Blessed Sacrament. Allow me, I beg you, to pray that you and I and all your people, reunited in the same faith and in the same Church, may one day receive the same crown.

We have here at least six hundred lepers, for whom the smallest help that you will send will be a real blessing. As for me, please understand that, having taken the vow of poverty, I need next to nothing.

May the eternal blessing of God be upon you, upon your family and on all who join with you in relieving my destitute children.

Affectionately yours,

J. Damien

Three months later, Chapman dispatched a donation of 975 pounds sterling, accompanied by these beautiful lines:

My dear Father,

You will find enclosed a little sum (almost $4,800.00) which some Christians have charged me with sending to you and which they will be grateful to you for accepting. The best way, they think, to please you and to bring back the smile to your lips, is to help you to comfort your lepers. They leave you absolutely free to dispense this money as you wish....

May this little flower of love that England sends you spread its perfume around you. May it be a sign to you of the affection of those who present it to you in the hope of meeting you in heaven.

Your friend who loves you,

Hugh B. Chapman

If it had been left to Chapman, the whole British Empire would have come to the aid of Father Damien. Not satisfied with writing in the *Tablet*, he also sent a letter to the editor of another London newspaper, the *Times*:

Sir,

An account of Father Damien's work and the heroic penalty which he has paid appeared not long ago in most of the papers. The case is as simple as it is sad. This manly priest, himself under a vow of poverty, lives on the island of Molokai, which is confined to lepers, among whom he has irretrievably cast his lot. He has himself fallen prey to the disease, and in a cheerful letter which he has lately written to me says that he would most gladly receive any contributions for his poor people. I have received the willing sympathy of his Eminence Cardinal Manning in the publication of his appeal and shall be happy to undertake all acknowledgments and transmission. The case speaks for itself, though I could have wished that it had a worthier channel of expression.

I am, sir, your obedient servant,

H. B. Chapman.

The *Times* printed the letter. It brought many donations. But Chapman's generous heart was still not satisfied:

> I wish I might offer you my personal services, but it is the will of God, I believe, that I remain with the poor among whom I live. Although I am myself too poor to assist them, I have not the heart to leave them. Were it not for this, I should have come in search of you and I should have taken care of you to the day you leave for heaven....
>
> I know that in your eyes I do not belong to the Church. Nothing, nevertheless, can hinder me from kneeling at your feet as a humble disciple before an eminent servant of God.
>
> Permit me to call myself your friend, your friend who loves you.
>
> H. B. Chapman

Edward Clifford

Clifford was an Englishman of artistic and cultivated tastes, who lived in comfortable circumstances and liked to employ his leisure at painting.

"One evening in the spring of 1887," Clifford relates, "I read an account of Father Damien in a magazine, and I made up my mind almost immediately that I would go and see him on the return from my next visit to the Indies. God knows that in my early days I had an aversion for the Roman Church and its priests. When I was a little boy, I thought that all Roman Catholics were wicked and went steadily to hell. If I saw a nun, I thought she wanted to catch me and burn me."

Clifford arrived at the leprosarium on December 17, 1888,

and stayed there two weeks. During the following month spent in Honolulu, he wrote his *Father Damien*, which was published a little later. The following is from this book:

> The sea was too rough for us to land at Kalaupapa. Finally, it was decided to put off a boat for a rocky point about a mile and a half distant from the village. From this point, I saw a dark figure in a large straw hat in the midst of about twenty lepers, slowly moving along the hillside. I chose a fit moment to leap ashore. Father Damien caught me by the hand and immediately called me: "Edward."
>
> At first glance, those white-washed cottages which are stretched out in the sunlight at the foot of the black pali make a pretty picture. Suddenly sadness grips you. They are in the valley of death. In those white cabins, like worms in a grave, leprosy is devouring its victims. One thinks of the whited sepulchers of the Gospel.

With much difficulty, the traveler brought ashore many gifts: some were gifts of money, others were gifts in kind.

> First, there came an engraving of Mr. Shield's "Good Shepherd" from Lady Mount Temple; then a set of large pictures of the Stations of the Cross, from the Hon. Maude Stanley; then a magic lantern with Scriptural slides; and finally a barrel organ which would play about forty tunes.... Most valuable of all, there was a watercolor painting of the Vision of St. Francis by Mr. Burne-Jones....
>
> On Christmas Day I gave him a copy of Faber's hymns, which had been sent to him by Lady Grosvenor's three children. He loved little children very much and told me with evident feeling that the book was a precious gift of which he would make frequent use.

Clifford was also thoughtful enough to have transported

from the Indies a large quantity of gurjun oil—a "wonder" oil used by lepers on the Andaman Islands and generally accepted as beneficial.

> I don't think Father Damien had much faith in the gurjun oil, but at my request he began using it, and after a fortnight's trial, the good effects became evident to all.

His lungs had become affected and his voice was hoarse. However, he forced himself to sing hymns to show that his voice was improving.

He consented, also, to pose for the artist. The sittings were held on the first-floor balcony of the priest-house.

> It was shaded by a honeysuckle in blossom. A door from it led to his sitting room...with its big map of the world.... Some of my happiest times on Molokai were spent on this little balcony.
>
> This man, thick-set, strongly-built, with curly black hair and short beard turning gray must have been handsome in earlier days.... But now he is disfigured by leprosy, though not so badly as to make it anything but a pleasure to look at his bright, sensible face. (Lately he had been able to sleep only with his mouth open.)
>
> He looked at my work mournfully. "What an ugly face!" he said. "I did not know the disease had made such progress." I proposed to send a photograph of the painting to his brother Pamphile. "No, don't do it; it would be too painful for him to see me like this."
>
> While I sketched him, he often read his breviary. At other times we talked about subjects that interested us both.... I need scarcely say that he gives himself no airs of martyr, saint, or hero—a humbler man I never saw.... One day I asked him if he would like to send a message to Cardinal Manning. He said that it was not for such as he

> to send a message to so great a dignitary; but after a moment's hesitation, he added, "I send my humble respects and thanks."
>
> He asked many affectionate questions about Mr. Hugh B. Chapman, who had shown him warm friendship and had sent him a large sum of money.
>
> I sang for him some English hymns, to two of which he took especially kindly: "Safe Home in Port" and "Brief Life Is Here Our Portion." At times the expression on his face was particularly sweet and tender....
>
> No sincere man could feel a real barrier in intercourse with one so good as Father Damien, and on his side he always showed a true and wholesome charity when he dealt with views which he considered erroneous. He was eager to demonstrate that his accounting for the gifts he received was in order and that the donations were distributed fairly among Catholics and non-Catholics.
>
> At his house, it was pleasant to see how happy and at home the lepers were.... I felt less horror than I expected at their strange aspect. There were generally several of them playing in the garden below us.

They ground out their music on the barrel organ of Lady Charteris.

When parting from this new friend, whom he would never see again, Father Damien gave him a card on which he had written: "To Edward Clifford from his leper friend, Joseph Damien de Veuster."

He then asked Clifford for his Bible; and in it he inscribed in a large hand: "I was sick and ye visited me."

As the steamer was carrying the artist away from Molokai, Clifford stood on the ship's bridge, waving farewell to Father Damien, who remained on the breakwater in the midst of his lepers.

Brother Joseph Dutton

Ira B. Dutton was forty-three when, on July 29, 1886, he landed at Kalaupapa. Although Damien was at the landing stage with old William to welcome lepers, he was not expecting Dutton. Respectfully saluting the priest, Dutton presented a paper signed by Hendry, secretary of the Board of Health, assigning him to the lazaretto as assistant to Dr. Mouritz.

"This newcomer," wrote the doctor, "was an impressive man, tall and well-knit. He had brown hair, grayish blue eyes, placid features and a pleasant smile. He was reserved and thoughtful, and he had nothing to say about his past life."

It was discovered later that he had been born on April 27, 1843, at Stowe, Vermont; that he had taken part as a volunteer in the Civil War; and that subsequently he had for four years been employed in the civil service of the United States.

He had married a wife who, not long after the wedding, proved unfaithful. In 1881, he instituted a divorce suit and won the case. The unfaithful partner did not even appear in court, so poor a defense did she seem to have. She died shortly thereafter.

To be fair, it should be added that at times the conduct of Dutton had left something to be desired. In 1883, however, grace touched his heart and he entered the Catholic Church on his fortieth birthday. Later he went to the Trappist Monastery of Our Lady of Gethsemani in Kentucky, as an oblate (i.e., a layman without any vows, free to leave at will). From that time to the day of his death, he led a life of extraordinary self-sacrifice.

Because active life was more to his taste than the contemplative life of the Trappists, Dutton left the shelter of Gethsemani after twenty months and went forth in quest of his true vocation. The book written by Charles W. Stoddard of Notre Dame University, *The Lepers of Molokai*, was instrumental in leading him to his life's work. He went to Janesville,

Wisconsin, to bid farewell to his mother; assigned to her a portion of his estate for her support; and set out for Honolulu by way of Memphis and San Francisco.

In the capital of the Hawaiian Islands, Dutton called upon the bishop, as well as Mr. and Mrs. Gibson, upon whom he made a very favorable impression. Eyeing Dutton's cheap blue suit, Mr. Gibson offered him wages for his proffered services on Molokai. Dutton declined to accept any remuneration. A lady at the Gibson home urged him to be more careful than Father Damien had been. Thanking them for their interest, he parted from them. Soon after, he sailed for Molokai, from which only death was to separate him.

For this "good companion" Father Damien blessed Providence. At first, Dutton took up his quarters in the priest-house; and for a year and a half he dined at the table of the leper-priest. Then he built a little cabin for himself nearby. Father Damien called him "Brother Joseph." Although always a layman, Dutton had some title to the "Brother," since he was a tertiary of St. Francis. The priest made him his sacristan, put him in charge of the boys' orphanage and laid a load of other chores on his shoulders.

Said Damien, smiling: "I am the carpenter, the man who does the heavy labor; you are the skilled artisan, who does delicate work to perfection."

"Father's head was swarming with ideas," explains Dutton, "and scarcely had one project been completed when he passed over to another that seemed more pressing than the first. He spoke to me of an up-to-date kitchen, a large bath house, a new church with which he wished to endow the leprosarium before he died. My role was to bring to a conclusion what he had started along his road. It was fortunate that I had handled tools before and had had experience in construction while in the army.

"At first, I had asked myself whether there would be enough to keep me busy at the lazaretto. I was quickly reassured. I arose at four-thirty in the morning and worked steadily until ten or eleven at night."

There seemed to be nothing that Brother Joseph could not put his hand to, nothing that he was unwilling to tackle. He accepted the most repulsive tasks, in imitation of the model he daily had before his eyes. Under the doctors' tutelage, he nursed the sick in their homes with his customary patience. In the long run, the patients preferred him to the doctors themselves. Discreet, frank, affable, cheerful in speech, he won and kept the good will of all the patients at the lazaretto. "Dutton had a divine temper; nothing could ruffle it," said Dr. Mouritz. This kindly tertiary of St. Francis was to serve the lepers of Molokai for forty-five years.

In January, 1889, Brother Joseph received a recognition that moved him deeply. From some bits of jewelry he had made a crucifix of solid gold. When completed, the cross was too beautiful for a tertiary in the service of lepers; hence, he offered it to the reigning Pope, Leo XIII. The Pontiff asked a Dr. O'Connell to convey his thanks for the gift. "After telling the Holy Father at length about your work," Dr. O'Connell wrote, "I was commissioned by the Holy Father to inform you that he sends to you, Brother Joseph, his Apostolic Blessing."

The contrast between these two brothers in heroism was striking. The former plowboy from Flanders was brusque in speech, impetuous of temperament and careless in appearance. The former army officer was neat of person, quiet of speech and ingratiating in manner.

Perhaps because they were complementary, they got along perfectly. "The good understanding between us was positive and genuine," wrote Dutton. "There was love between us. This is not to say that our tastes and personal habits were the same.... (But) I was firm in one resolve—to get along with everyone and everything." In 1906, he wrote, "If in the twenty years I have been on Molokai I cannot be charged with having broken that resolution in any significant manner, it is due to no particular virtue on my part, but rather to the grace that God accorded me in giving me the Faith."

During the evenings they spent together in the early days, Father Damien often suggested that Dutton go on to the priesthood, so that he could step into the former's shoes after death had taken him. "Had I been fit," wrote Dutton, "it might have been different. But the priesthood requires high character and great purity. I was not fit to be a priest or under vows and serve at the altar, and his request bothered me greatly.... I could not, for certain reasons, tell him why I was not fit to become a priest. Later, however, I did. He at once ceased speaking about it." Confidence for confidence, Damien told him his own story of how he had left the plow to become a missionary in the Hawaiian Islands.

This was the only vexation of mind that Dutton experienced, unless we should include the efforts of well-intentioned friends to get him to take a vacation trip away from Molokai. "Seek a vacation?" he replied. "Why, I have a vacation all the time, every blessed minute of the time, every moment of all these blessed years, in doing what I like, what I think my soul needs.... The people here like me, I think, and I am sure I like them."

As long as Father Damien lived, Dutton made an annual vow "to serve the Catholic Mission at the Asylum on Molokai," a pledge which placed him under the jurisdiction of the Bishop of Honolulu. In later years, after the coming of sisters and brothers to Molokai, he pursued his work without vows, solely under the direction of the Board of Health, but keeping the memory of the leper priest green and intact.

Dutton himself became a personage of note. Several presidents of the United States wrote to him out of respect for his work. Edison, the inventor, sent a fine phonograph and a set of records as a gift for his orphans.

During the day, Dutton devoted himself entirely to his sick and his orphans; in the evenings he remained at home to pray, to study books on medicine and botany, to write letters or brief articles and later to arrange material for his memoirs. He had heard so many groundless stories spread to discredit Father Damien that he probably feared being vilified in his turn, after death would make it impossible to reply. He left after him pounds and pounds of neat, handwritten notes. From these records, a nephew wrote a detailed biography. In addition to events which have been alluded to above, these notes recorded gifts totaling about $10,000 that Dutton had made to the leprosarium and a statement of the medical expenses he had incurred in treating a highly prized horse that had fallen ill.

Only once was Brother Joseph tempted to leave the lazaretto for a time. This was at the moment when the United States decided to enter the first world war. Dutton dreamed of organizing a veterans' company "to give an example to younger men." Of his former comfortable estate, little now remained. In addition to subscribing to war bonds, he gave the government a pair of binoculars, practically the only private possession still in his hands. Franklin Delano Roosevelt, in those days Assistant Secretary of the Navy, sent him a letter of thanks in which he named the ship to which the binoculars had been issued. After the armistice, the old gentleman received an official certificate attesting the wartime service rendered by his gift. He rejoiced in having had some little part in the victory of his country.

When Mother Marianne and he chanced to meet in their later years, they joked about death's seeming forgetfulness of the two of them; and they speculated about who should be first to bring to Father Damien in the other world, the latest news about his lazaretto. Actually, the mother superior went first to that other world. Mother Marianne died in 1918; and at a cost of $600.00 Dutton raised a monument stone over her grave.

Brother Joseph's own sturdy health remained with him

until 1928. In that year began the decline which ended in his death on March 26, 1931.

James Sinnet

"Brother" James Sinnet spent only eight months with Father Damien, but they were the last months of the apostle's life.

That Irishman had knocked about the world without giving much edification anywhere – until he came to his journey's end at Molokai.

By way of expiation for his stormy career, Sinnet signed up for work as a hospital orderly under the Board of Health. Since he was at that time penniless in St. Louis, Missouri, he had to have his fare from St. Louis to Honolulu advanced to him. After his arrival on Molokai, he became a model of faithful industry. It was he who took personal care of Father Damien in the last stages of his illness and closed his eyes in death.

Immediately upon Sinnet's arrival, the priest named him "Brother James" and made him assistant to "Brother Joseph" in the management of the boys' orphanage.

When the author Stevenson visited that orphanage after Damien's death, he remarked that its state of cleanliness was "superficial" and the system of lighting and ventilating less advanced than that used in the sanatoria of England. He noted a certain nonchalance and some shabbiness.

Even the more fastidious lepers would make remarks about this orphanage, and, when pressed, Father Damien would admit that there was some truth in the innuendoes. He had managed according to the means at his disposal and under the pressure of urgent need. Things would improve with time. Sometimes Brother Joseph and Brother James had to swim beyond their depth. Even with their combined knowledge of pedagogy and bookkeeping, they were not in the first rank of administrators.

"After all, it could be worse, couldn't it?" said Dutton to Stevenson. "Besides, we are marking time until the sisters come. They will put everything in order. Then you will see things hum!"

When Damien's hand was no longer able to hold his pen, Sinnet acted as his secretary.

Edward Clifford was still in Honolulu on January 4, 1889, when Sinnet sent him this news about the dying man:

"I sometimes offend Father Damien's modesty by telling him he is appearing younger and better looking since using your oil of gurjun.... Father Damien requests that when you write home to Rev. Mr. Chapman you will express his unbounded gratitude to that zealous friend of the lepers and all others associated with him in the good work."

With his own hand, Damien added a postscript to Sinnet's letter: "Being very busy, I endorse everything Brother James says. *Au revoir*. The Lord bless you, J. Damien."

A month and a half later, another letter came to Clifford from Sinnet, to which Father Damien again contributed a postscript: "My love and good wishes to good friend Edward. I try to make slowly my Way of the Cross and hope to reach the summit of my Golgotha. Yours forever, J. Damien."

The good-hearted Clifford was chagrined to realize that his oil of gurjun had failed to cure his friend. "Since he is doomed to death," he wrote Brother James, "read to him from Father Faber's book that I brought him the chapter entitled, 'The Will of God and Christian Perfection.'"

Counsel for counsel, Father Damien escorted Clifford by return courier: "During your traveling on the long journey homewards, please do not forget the narrow road. We both have to walk carefully, so as to meet together at the home of our common and eternal Father.... *Bon voyage, mon cher ami, et au revoir au ciel*. Devotedly yours, J. Damien."

Clifford received a final letter from Sinnet dated July,

1889. By that time, Father Damien had been dead for three months. "I regret to say that there has been an outbreak of intemperance among the lepers," Sinnet remarked. "The salutary fear of a Damien kept the wrong-doers in check; but illicit distilling has begun again now; and, as I write, three well-armed men are barricaded in their house, refusing to submit to a sentence of three months' hard labor for distilling."

Sinnet did not stay long to witness renewals of such spectacles. His great friend, Father Damien, was no longer there to sustain his resolution. He concluded that his position at the leprosarium was now untenable; and it was not long before he informed Clifford that he was quitting Molokai for good. What ultimately became of him, we do not know.

Lambert Conrardy

May 17, 1888, was one of the memorable days in the life of Father Damien. Rarely was he as happy as on the day he saw Abbé Conrardy coming ashore to stay with him.

During the three years that had preceded this day, Damien had felt as if he were walled up alive. Was he destined to die without spiritual assistance, without the ministrations of a priest? But now he welcomed a compatriot from whom he would never be separated—more than a friend, a good-natured and stouthearted brother.

Abbé Conrardy was a native of the Walloon section of Belgium. He was born at Liege on July 12, 1841; he studied under the Jesuits; he was ordained a priest on June 15, 1866, and exercised his early ministry in his own diocese.

In the epidemic of 1866, he was a curate at Stavelot where, forgetful of his own safety, he nursed the poor with his own hands and gave them all he possessed, including his own bed.

He was a man marked by faith, charity and extraordinary courage, a man who would accept martyrdom as the surest road to heaven. As opportunities for dying for the Faith seemed to be rare in Belgium at that time, he left his country and began his quest, destined to extend over the greater part of the globe, for perilous tasks and challenging assignments.

The year 1871 found him in Paris, making one plea after another for assignment to the China missions. He fell somewhat short of his mark, getting only as far as a mission in India. After two or three years among the Hindus, he appeared in America, bringing the Gospel to the Indians in the Rocky Mountains. In those open vastnesses he could give free rein to his pastoral zeal, even in the face of unmistakable peril. He remained in his trackless Oregon parish for fifteen years.

It was so large a parish that, in those days, it took three months to cross it. He traveled about on foot or on horseback, in fair weather, in rain, in snow, with no weapons—not even a knife. He was devoid of fear, and the Indians knew it.

One day, a chief came to him with the cheerful news that, since it was clear that he had no fear of being scalped, they were going to hang him! Conrardy gravely took out his watch.

"Take this," he said to the chief. "Since you have the kindness to offer to hang me, I must respond with a gift for you."

The chief was nonplused at this unexpected offer. Asking for time to think it over, he went to consult the elders of the tribe. They advised letting him go his way—this mysterious fellow who wished to sacrifice his watch for the pleasure of being hanged.

After Conrardy had experienced several equally hair-raising adventures and had cured some of the sick, he was treated with respect on all sides.

Danger did not disturb Father Conrardy's equable temper, nor even privation of the necessities of life. He was so destitute in his mountain parish that he made potatoes serve as candle-holders during Mass; after Mass, he would boil and eat these candlesticks, having nothing else in the larder.

Even into this rocky vastness, word about Molokai managed to penetrate. It came in the form of a letter printed in the *Annals of the Propagation of Faith*, in which Father Damien expressed his regret over his inability to meet all the demands of his apostolate among the lepers. Without delay, the apostle of the Indians wrote, offering to help the apostle of the Lepers. The exchange of letters planted the seeds of friendship which later came to fruition on Molokai.

The first letters in this correspondence are not extant. Perhaps Damien looked upon the coming of Conrardy as wishful thinking. Certainly, his superiors were cold regarding the idea.

As a rule, it is prudent to have the personnel of a mission homogeneous. If possible, the priests serving at a mission should be members of the same congregation, submitting to the same rule and the same superiors, being liable to the same sanctions.

This common practice was being respected in Oregon at the time, as the following letter from Father Conrardy indicates: "I have spent thirteen years among these Indians. Do you want me, my dear compatriot? I have in me the ability to work for twenty years more, at the least. My bishop has just entrusted this mission to the Jesuits. If I do not go to Molokai, I shall have to join the Jesuits in order to remain here."

Conrardy had no intention of entering the Society of Jesus. He preferred to keep his independence and to fight as a sharpshooter on the skirmish line.

As events proved, his vocation really was to serve the lepers. Actually, his superior in Oregon, Archbishop Groos, encouraged him to go to Hawaii. You may recall Bishop Groos as the "American business agent of the lepers."

Damien, who felt more abandoned than ever just a year

before his death, did not conceal his yearning for his Belgian fellow-priest.

The bishop of Honolulu, however, made some stipulations. For example, at the very outset Father Conrardy would have to agree to enter the Picpus Congregation. He readily gave his promise. Thereupon, the bishop wrote a letter informing Conrardy that he might come.

"That he might come..." in order to start his novitiate, after which he could go to Molokai. Conrardy was not receptive to this proposal, and he replied that he wished to go straight to the lazaretto, with the way left open to become a Picpus Father later on – in four years' time perhaps.

The bishop was in a quandary. This counterproposal was not in accordance with regulations. Damien entered the plea that to leave him, a condemned man, without proper assistance, would be an even graver infraction of rules. He added the argument that since his case was unique, the bishop could quite fittingly authorize a secular priest to be his companion.

The bishop yielded to these pleas and invited Father Conrardy to come without further delay. A little later, he had some misgivings, but he hesitated to reverse himself. Besides, it was too late to do anything: Father Conrardy was *en route*. "I shall be in Honolulu on the tenth of May," he announced.

The bishop then wrote to Damien, "I make you responsible for whatever happens." In a letter to the general, he said: "With this unknown priest, the mutual understanding (at Molokai) will be perfect in the beginning. But will it last? It will last just long enough, probably, to fill the world with the glory of the Belgians to the disadvantage of the congregation and the Mission."

The bishop had made many prophecies. This time, the latter part of this prophecy just missed coming to pass.

Was it Conrardy's fault? He was quite effusive, not at all reticent about his affairs. While in Honolulu, he was indiscreet enough to show a newspaperman the letter in which Damien begged him to come. The letter was published; and on May 17, a secular gazette rang with praise of the Belgian priest who had come rushing from Oregon to assist a forsaken fellow-countryman. It was easy to read between the lines that the priest from America might not have found it necessary to take so long a journey if the Picpus Fathers, who were quite close at hand, had come to Damien's aid.

This publicity constituted an open affront to the Mission. The provincial wrote to Father Damien, "In this affair in which you have so rashly enmeshed yourself with your compatriot, you have succeeded in offending, yes insulting, your confreres."

As a step toward repairing the damage, the bishop addressed a circular to all his missionaries, asking them if they were ready to go to Molokai. All replied in the affirmative. This reply was publicized; and if people of ill-will still harped upon the past deficiencies of the missionaries, at least there was no excuse for denying their current good disposition.

Need it be remarked, then, that no matter what Conrardy's role in all this, the priest from Wallonia was regarded at first with something less than enthusiasm by the Picpus superiors in Honolulu?

There was some thought of getting rid of him. "My impression of him is not very favorable," wrote the bishop to the general on June 1. "He is full of himself and is inclined to drink."

The basis for his statement was that while Conrardy was being welcomed at the house of the Picpus sisters, he had asked for a second glass of table wine. Perhaps the sisters had been a bit thrifty in pouring his first glass, and he surely was entitled to revive his spirits after fifteen years of privation among the Indians. As a matter of fact, Conrardy was as sober as his critics, and the loquacious little sister who talked about him had been too eager to retail a bit of information.

Archbishop Groos gave the Abbé this testimonial: "He is a

man of upright and heroic character. Like me, he has covered the whole of Oregon on foot. His life of privation has been a perfect preparation for the life he will lead on Molokai. Since he is aware that, sooner or later, he will fall a victim himself, it is an act of true heroism he is performing in going there of his own free will."

Damien was charmed with his new assistant. "He is a veteran missionary who is clearly at home here," he wrote to the superior general. "He has done me many a good turn in the two months that, like a cheerful brother and a kind companion, he has been at my side, leper though I am. He has already begun to speak Kanaka. We must find some way of keeping him here without requiring him to go to Europe for his novitiate."

The general had the humanity and wisdom to agree with Damien and to prevail upon the superiors in Honolulu to leave the Abbé undisturbed at the lazaretto.

Besides, the complexion of the affair had changed. "He is a perfect gem," wrote the bishop in September. "He is a real treasure," said the provincial, going the bishop one better.

Conrardy was truly an angel of consolation, "the friend and the real brother of Father Damien," as Sister St. Vincent declared, having surprised him one day in tears at the bedside of the leper priest.

Father Conrardy had his quarters and ate his meals in the priest-house at Kalawao. "Shall I escape contagion?" he asked in a letter. "Humanly speaking, it is impossible, I believe. Our cooks are lepers, and lepers bake our bread. At table, I sit near Father Damien. In the beginning, the mere sight of him drove away my appetite. I suffered without let up from headaches. At present, I am used to it all.... I can only say, 'God shield me!' and ask my friends to pray that I may persevere in my endeavor."

Damien went out of his way to spoil him: "Often he would bring me an orange or some tidbit. 'Here,' said he, 'eat this. It will do you good. And don't worry: no leper has touched it,' forgetting that he himself, covered with horrible sores, is a leper from head to foot....

"What man was Father Damien! How active! How forgetful of self and how kind! I swore never to leave him."

After Damien's death, Conrardy stayed six years longer on Molokai. In 1895, since he did not have a vocation for the Picpus Congregation, and since through American help the leprosarium was no longer in great need, he set out for China in search of lepers who were really abandoned.

He discovered some living in appalling misery in the neighborhood of Canton. No one bothered about them except to consign their bodies to the flames, sometimes before life had become extinct. The Abbé decided to adopt them all as his children. He planned to gather them together on a tiny island. First, however, he had to do two things: collect funds to purchase the island, and become a physician in order to comply with the requirements of the Chinese authorities.

At the age of fifty-five, the veteran missionary returned to school. From 1896 to 1900 he could be found among the students in the lecture halls of the University of Portland, Oregon.

After he had at length won his diploma as a doctor of medicine, he went to Europe on a begging tour. His letters show that he went to Rome, to Paris, to Belgium, to England – giving sermons and lectures, visiting homes with his hand stretched out, publicizing his appeal through newspapers. Misfortunes often disheartened him; he fell ill after he had been arrested as an alleged swindler; at times he was reduced to tears; but he never surrendered his determination to see his project through. "If God permits me to spend ten years in China, I shall be a happy man," he wrote. "I have prayed to get the most horrible place in the world; I know that I shall have it in the near future."

On his final quest for financial aid, he traveled through Canada and the United States. At long last, he got back to

China, in May, 1908, with a bank balance of about $30,000. The island of Shek-Lung off Canton he judged to be a suitable site for his purpose. He bought about fifty acres of land, put up some wooden cabins and went forth to gather in his lepers.

At first he had seventy sick people on his hands, with no assistants and with unforeseen difficulties and dangers besetting his path. However, with his combination of tenacity and medical skill, he achieved prodigious results. In 1913, the Chinese government gave the settlement its approbation and support; hence, when the Abbé died in the following year, the future of Shek-Lung was assured. At that time, seven hundred sick persons were sheltered in a settlement—directed by two priests and five sisters—which was considered the equal of Molokai at its best.

After the Abbé's death, his lepers were loud in his praise. "Make no mistake, the sun has never shone on another man like Dr. Conrardy. We are ten times more indebted to him than to our own fathers."

They had seen the Abbé kneel at their feet to wash their sores and mingle his tears with their own in his efforts to comfort them. "Courage, my friend! Soon you will be as beautiful as an angel and happy forever!" He never parted from them without embracing them. When his co-worker, Father Deswazieres, remonstrated and begged him to be prudent, the Abbé replied, "Leprosy would be the finest decoration I could receive. But alas! I am not worthy!"

It was not from Hansen's disease but from pneumonia that he died on August 2, 1914. In accordance with his wishes, he was buried, rolled in a mat, between two lepers.

Chapter 15

Trials

In the last years of his life, Damien endured trials infinitely more cruel than all his preceding misfortunes.

The hostility he encountered had its source in Honolulu. There were men in that capital city whom his success disconcerted and provoked; there were also persons who misunderstood the priest of Molokai. Among these were Damien's religious superiors.

In secular affairs, a subordinate who finds his superior officer unsympathetic can find some way out of a vexatious situation. In the religious life, however, the subordinate is inhibited by his vow of obedience, in accordance with which he renounces his own will and obeys God in the person of his superior. The sufferings of such a subordinate can be imagined when the wielders of authority are deficient in understanding, tact and kindly appreciation.

A Change of Leadership

So long as Damien had Louis Maigret as his bishop and Father Modeste as his provincial, his affairs flowed along with tolerable smoothness. Those two men had a genuine sympathy for him, and they recognized his progress against heavy odds, even though they sometimes found it necessary to moderate his zeal. But the picture changed when these two were taken from the scene. Father Regis was made assistant to Father Modeste in 1878, and in 1883, Father "L" took over the office of provincial. In 1881 Bishop Maigret was assigned an auxiliary, Bishop Kockeman, who shortly afterwards succeeded him as Bishop of Honolulu. Like all other men, these three were a mixture of virtues and failings.

Damien had his own shortcomings, chief among them the tendency to see only the interests of his lepers and the propensity to speak and act with brusqueness and obstinacy. His superiors, on their part, were absorbed in caring for the general interests of the Mission, and they had little leisure to deal calmly and patiently with the difficulties that were inevitable in Damien's complex apostolate. It is clear, at any rate, that during Damien's lifetime these three failed to understand and appreciate this extraordinary man.

"He is a man almost completely wanting in judgment," Father Regis wrote to the superior general in 1879. And again in 1880: "He needs a guardian; he is ineffective as a priest; he has no head; he is ill-mannered."

Father Regis was incorrect on these points. Undoubtedly, like all other mortals, Damien made his mistakes; but it was his humility that allowed him to recognize them as such, and his good judgment that persuaded him to rectify them.

As for Damien's "need of a guardian," his work on Molokai was precisely that of a guardian.

An ineffective priest? May God grant the Church many such, for Damien made religion appealing, and his witness led others to a similar heroism.

As for his manners, it should suffice to point out that the visitors who came from the outside world to the lazaretto were charmed by his kindness and some became his good friends.

When Father "L" became provincial, he was no more favorable to Damien than Father Regis had been. "He is an overbearing man, capricious and proud," he wrote. "He has led people to regard him as the consoler and the nurse, etc., of the lepers; and he is nothing of the sort." Again in 1888: "The worst of all our missionaries is Father Damien, who has been lifted so high by adulation that no one henceforth will succeed in getting him down to earth again."

The new bishop was scarcely less reserved in his remarks: "Our celebrated hero of Molokai," he wrote in 1887, "has received so many compliments that he seems to be in danger of losing the balance of his judgment."

It is only right to record that the testimony of unimpeachable witnesses supports the view that Father Damien was very humble. He suffered great embarrassment when he found that his name was beginning to appear in the secular press, in consequence of the publication of one of his letters. He made it a point to let those he considered responsible feel his displeasure. "I have not answered your letter before this," he wrote to his parents in 1876, "because I have been very much annoyed by the insertion of my last letter in the *Annals*. Now I am spoken of as far away as America. Once and for all, please understand that I do not like this at all. I wish to remain unknown to the world."

There was no one less interested than he in promoting his own renown. Fame came to him, as to many others, quite by chance. If he accepted his being a celebrity, as he accepted his being a beggar, a bookkeeper, a grave-digger and a leper, it was only for the good he hoped to bring to his sick people. He would have agreed to be anything within reason, provided his "children" might profit from it. When he understood that, in speaking of him, the press of the world was serving his lepers, he let it speak; just as he would have wanted it silent, if its silence would have conferred more benefit on them.

The publicity stirred up a most bitter enmity against him.

When it was discovered in Honolulu that the foreign press was organizing campaigns for donations in his interest, a tumult arose among the newspapers of the political party opposed to the administration, and anger mounted in government circles.

It should be observed that in this period between 1880 and 1895, the Hawaiian Islands were anticipating their inevitable annexation by the United States; and in these unsettled years, they were the victims of virulent political strife.

With an indignation that was, perhaps, feigned, the journals of the opposition cried out, "One thing is clear: either the sums of money that come to Damien are necessary, or they are not. If they are necessary, this means that the Board of Health—i.e. the government—which has charge of maintaining the leprosarium is not giving it proper support; or else the Board harbors grafters who steal and enrich themselves at the lepers' expense.

"If these sums of money are not necessary, then what is the meaning of these fraudulent appeals to English and American charity? Are they not designed to refill the treasury of the Mission? It is up to the government to put an end to all these proceedings and, as a means of preventing abuses, to place squarely on the Board the responsibility for receiving and distributing all donations.

"In either case, the government has been delinquent and the honor of Hawaii has been compromised."

The government's embarrassment can be imagined. Its spokesman revealed that an appropriation of $100,000 a month was made for the leprosarium; and he gave as satisfactory a proof as possible that the money was honestly expended.

Replies made by men in office, however, rarely convince opponents who live in the hope of supplanting them. The political warfare continued, and as time went on it became obvious that each side had it in for the Mission. The opposition questioned the fairness of the Picpus priests; the incumbents considered the Mission responsible for drawing them into this mischievous affair.

The superiors of the Mission lost their heads. They saw the specter of revolution rise, and they feared for the Mission's continued existence. "A change in administration is to be feared which will put enemies of the missionaries into office," wrote the provincial to the general. "I am afraid there may be bloodshed." For his part, the bishop wrote to Damien, "The administration may change. We must be prepared for anything. See what is going on at this very moment in the hospitals of Paris!"

As a matter of fact, none of the things they feared happened in Hawaii. But both the bishop and the provincial had bungled an opportunity to reply appropriately to their opponents.

Instead of defending their soldier in the field, Damien's superiors addressed to him seven strictures:

> 1. In addition to other sizable gifts, you have received from America $28,621.00 – thanks to your letters, in which you have exaggerated the wretchedness of the lepers and have ventured to criticize the government. In this way, you have given grievous offense to the king and to Mr. Gibson, his prime minister. Henceforth, under obedience you will send all your correspondence through Father "L", who will censor it.
>
> 2. You have been making unwarranted boasts that you are "a man of thirty-six different trades": nurse, carpenter, grave-digger, etc. – as if you were the only one at the lazaretto capable of doing any work.
>
> 3. The newspapers have praise only for you. They pass over in silence the part played by the government.
>
> 4. The newspapers never mention the Mission.
>
> 5. Nine hundred and seventy-five pounds sterling have come to you from England. What shall you say if

some jealous enemy reproaches you with having solicited that money under false pretenses?

6. Keep your checks. I (Father "L") wish to have nothing to do with your money. However, I do put you under obedience to make at once a will in favor of the bishop or his successor.

7. You are the occasion, if not the cause, of the plan of some non-Catholic sisters to set up an establishment at the lazaretto.

In the face of his accusers, Father Damien bore himself like a saint. Insofar as he felt that he could pour oil on ruffled waters, he defended himself in moderate terms. When he saw that argument only resulted in irritation and that his effort was vain, he grew silent. He continued to correspond with his accusers with simplicity and forbearance. Neither obsequious nor curt, he acted as though the whole matter were of little importance. He organized no defense and confided his troubles to no one – neither to his friends among the laity, nor to his confreres in the congregation, nor to Pamphile, nor even to his higher superiors, to whom he had the right to appeal. As for his beloved congregation, he preserved inviolate all his gratitude to it and deep affection for it.

But he must have found it cruel beyond telling to be condemned by those whom he regarded as interpreters for him of the will of God.

"You ask me again," he wrote to the provincial in 1883, "to answer your letter in which you express lack of confidence in me; and to keep quiet, not breathing even a word, while you find fault with me for considering myself above you in dignity and in achievement.

"I repeat that I have not opposed the coming of the sisters to the lazaretto. I have said nothing, written nothing to warrant that assumption. I simply thought that the project had been dropped.

"If the mother superior and one of her sisters will come to visit the leprosarium in Your Reverence's company, I will sweep out my house and see to it that all three of you are properly lodged. On that day, if my presence will displease you and you will let me know in time, I will find ways of keeping out of sight. I must confess that I did not believe I had fallen so low in the estimation of my superiors."

A Period of Anguish

In the face of the chorus of condemnation arising from those who in his eyes represented God, he took stock of his position. Had he deceived himself? Had he taken the wrong road? Had his active and impulsive temperament led him to entertain delusions? Had his "weak judgment and pride" tempted him to undertake a work contrary to the will of God? His death was not far away. At the judgment seat of God would he not meet the same condemnation he had received from his superiors?

It is quite easy to picture the mental torture suffered by this solitary man, isolated from his brethren and weakened by the ravages of his leprosy.

So heavy was his burden of fatigue and discouragement that at times he could almost wish his leprosy were more rapid in its progress. "I am not long for this cheerless world," he wrote. "I hope a layer of green turf will soon lie over my corpse."

Those who had the opportunity to observe Father Damien were at a loss to explain the depths of depression into which, despite his natural cheerfulness, he so often sank. The resident physician, Dr. Mouritz, considered him to be subject to scrupulosity, marked by "the fixed idea that he was unworthy of heaven."

It was tragic that Damien was deprived of a priest who

could have heard his confession and dispelled his anxieties.

At this time, Father Damien was more rigorously quarantined than any of his lepers. The mental and spiritual torments occasioned by this isolation began with the departure of Father Albert from Molokai in 1885. The following year he wrote to his former companion: "If you saw me in tears when you were leaving me, lay it to my sorrow at losing you and also to a presentiment of the solitude in which I should be doomed to spend the rest of my days."

Although he had immediately asked for a priest to replace Father Albert in accordance with article 392 of the Picpus Rule, no priest had come.

Since the leper priest could not have a companion to live with him, couldn't he at least be permitted to go to Honolulu when he wished to confess? It was only a four-hour sail from Molokai. But he was formally forbidden to do so by his provincial. The reason for this order was fear that the sick priest might sow contagion, spread terror among the people and cause the Mission headquarters to be placed under quarantine. It might be added that in January, 1885, precisely at the time the signs of leprosy broke out on Father Damien, the provincial council had decreed that leper priests were not to risk contaminating their confreres.

Damien suffered the consequences. In October of that same year, 1885, he wrote to his bishop: "Concurrently, as my disease advances, I am more and more blessed. But being without a good confessor is more difficult to bear than all the rest." And two months later, he lamented: "I am sometimes tempted to murmur against the somewhat tyrannical way in which this good Father is set on imprisoning me here. Yet, I am reluctant to lodge a complaint with the superior general. Pray for me."

Did he actually enter an appeal? We are inclined to think that it was the bishop who out of pity took the initiative in Damien's interest. When the father general learned of the situation, he directed that the sequestered priest be permitted to go to Honolulu for confession whenever he wished. Unfortunately, that permission did not reach Damien until 1887, by which time he was unable to take advantage of it.

In the meantime, nevertheless, he begged the provincial to come to his aid. But the provincial did not act, for he did not think he could. He replied to Damien on February 2, 1886: "Be patient. It is my duty to remind you of the decisions taken by the provincial council and not by me."

Damien was abandoned in complete desolation. He was forbidden to leave the island. Couldn't a visitor, at least, be permitted to drop in? "I am a leper, praise God!" he wrote to the provincial. "But as a favor—it is the only one I ask—let someone come down once a month into my grave to hear my confession!"

Occasionally, one priest did visit him: "Good Father Columban comes every two or three months to hear my confession and then hastens away again. I am at a loss to know how it will all end; but I am resigned. At the foot of the altar I confess and seek peace of mind. Before the tabernacle and the statue of the Blessed Virgin from time to time I whisper...."

It is opportune to recall what the spirit of faith discovers in similar experiences. God, who did not spare his own Son, does not show greater tenderness toward his best friends, the saints, who have all undergone intense sufferings here below. Indeed, some saints, such as John of the Cross, Alphonsus de Liguori, Therese of Lisieux and Bernadette of Lourdes, have received some of their keenest sufferings from the hands of their superiors. There is no reason for surprise, then, that—like other servants of God—Damien should have been subjected to the operations of that mystical dispensation of Providence. It is edifying to think that in imitation of the example of the saints, he had the humility to shoulder his cross and the perseverance to carry it to the end of the road.

Disobedience?

One day, however, a scheme for escaping from his prison insinuated itself into his mind. It is difficult to decide whether or not it led him to the brink of an act of disobedience.

It is, of course, a matter of fact that he was normally very submissive and most rigorous in interpreting the vow of obedience. In his *Spiritual Notebook*, he had written: "Be exact in following the smallest direction and prescription. Death to every movement of self-will! Let us, like so many corpses, allow the superiors to dispose of us as they judge best."

In 1878, he had asked his superior for permission to follow his own judgment if a matter should come up requiring him to act before he had time to ask for a decision: "Thus, I should no longer be exposed to scruples of conscience."

Now, at the beginning of the year 1886, he had good reasons for wishing to go to Honolulu. In his own interest, and even more in the interest of his lepers, he desired to study the Japanese treatment of leprosy recently introduced at Kakaako; even more earnestly, he wanted to go to confession.

Father "L" announced his opposition to the plan: "Please recall the decisions of the provincial council. Let me inform you, furthermore, that the bishop and the prime minister are opposed to this trip. Finally, in case you should leave the island, I forewarn you that you will have to go either to the Mission or to Kakaako.

"At the Mission you will be confined in a room which you will leave only to depart again for Molokai. If people learn that there is a leper in our house, they will take pains to avoid us and the Mission will be placed under quarantine. In a word, you will understand why it is impossible for you to study the regimen of Dr. Goto.

"If, on the other hand, you go to Kakaako, you will stay there without saying Mass, for neither Father Clement nor will I consent to celebrate with the chalice and other liturgical objects used by you; nor will the sisters consent to receive Communion from your hand."

Commenting on this letter, Damien wrote: "In the tone of a policeman rather than a religious superior, he repeated his prohibition." And Damien added: "This gave me the most bitter suffering I have had to endure at any time in my life."

But, as he wrote on June 16, "In virtue of my vow of obedience, I replied with an act of perfect submission."

At that date, then, he had made up his mind to forego the trip to Honolulu, despite the fact that Dr. Mouritz, alarmed by the advance of Damien's leprosy, had advised him to consult Dr. Goto.

Several sources make it clear that on July 2 he had not wavered from his resolve.

On July 8, however, he unexpectedly changed his views; and on July 10, he took ship for Honolulu.

What had happened?

Three documents throw some light on the situation. The first is a letter dated July 2, in which Damien asked the bishop to try to bend the provincial. The second is the bishop's reply, in which he informed Father Damien that Father "L" had raised the ban. The provincial had yielded with bad grace, however, for he had added, "So be it! But if he comes, he will have to bear the responsibility for whatever happens."

The third document is a letter from Mr. Meyer to Father Damien. The thoughtful superintendent had called on Prime Minister Gibson and on the formidable Father "L." After interceding for his friend, Father Damien, he wrote on July 8 to tell him, "The head of the government, whose permission you need to go to Honolulu, neither gives it nor refuses it." In this fashion, Gibson, whom the opposition party was giving a difficult time, left the way open in the event of unpleasant consequences, to say that he had no responsibility in the matter. "I have also seen

Father "L," upon whom I pressed the urgency of your trip. He had been of the opinion that the prime minister was adamant. I dispelled the illusion; thereupon he seemed to accept my view. In my judgment, it is your moral obligation to set out on your trip."

Damien's conscience was now pacified, and he set forth.

It was the last time that he was to sail from Molokai—the last time that he was to see his bishop, and King Kalakaua and his old friend, Prime Minister Gibson, all three of whom came to visit him in the hospital at Kakaako. He stayed at the hospital four or five days, taking Dr. Goto's treatment, edifying the Franciscan sisters who administered the institution and devoting his free time to the other patients. "I had the happiness of caring for him," recounted Sister Crescentia. "His mere presence warmed the heart, because we knew all that he had accomplished. He spoke only of his lepers, never of himself. He edified us by his cheerful patience."

Father Damien also saw his loyal benefactor, Mother Judith, the superior of the Picpus Sisters. To that old friend he whispered about the interior martyrdom he had endured. At one point, he even talked with her about the possibility of accepting the sisters' offer to allow him to spend his remaining days at Kakaako. "He had had as much as he could bear. Then I showed him the linens and the comforts I had gotten ready for his lepers. That was all it took to cheer him up. Without much delay, he loaded himself with bundles of these gifts and started back toward Molokai with joy in his heart."

A month afterward, in a letter to the father general, Father Damien described the Corpus Christi celebration that had just taken place at the lazaretto: "This time, I avoided my besetting sin of preaching too long. I gave a brief sermon, after which the procession was formed, more beautiful than ever." In this letter Damien also mentioned his trip to Honolulu, but without rating it as any more significant than the other events he recorded.

It is worthy of note, therefore, that six months after the

event, he should on December 30 hark back to that trip to Honolulu. In the report that he submitted at the close of the year, he wrote to Father Janvier, secretary to the general: "Now a word very unpleasant for me to say and, perhaps, for the good heart of our beloved Very Reverend Father General to receive.... Last July, after I had not set eyes on a confrere for about three months, I slipped away, almost (it is Damien who underlined the word) contrary to obedience; and I went to Honolulu where I had the consolation of going to confession to the bishop."

This letter, too lengthy to be quoted in full, saddens the compassionate heart. The harassed priest protested that he wished to remain "a son completely submissive and a sick man fully resigned to his lot." He spoke of his sequestration as more distressing than his disease; he asked that they pray and get others to pray that the good Lord confirm him in grace, since for three months he had not confessed and did not know when a confessor would come to him again. Apart from this vexation, he said, he was "happy and content," with "no complaint against anyone" and "leper or not, wish to end my days at Kalawao."

In walking humbly with his crushing load of scruples through the valley of mental anguish, Father Damien had trudged far along the road to perfection.

Chapter 16

The Testimony of R. L. S.

Father Damien's reputation, particularly in the sacred area of his priestly integrity, also had to weather a storm of vilification – with the angriest gale howling after his death.

This calumny came from a former sacristan of his. The man had paid court to a leper's widow who served in the priest-house preparing Father Damien's meals, supervised the girls in his orphanage, milked the cows in his stable, etc. She disdained the attention of the sacristan-suitor, who was not quite to her taste. He thereupon took revenge by slandering both the widow and the priest by whom she was employed.

This slander was later communicated to the press by Dr. C. M. Hyde.

Dr. Hyde, doctor of theology, "a refined, learned and charitable man" (in the words of Dr. Mouritz, who this time was a bit hasty in his judgment), taught philosophy to certain aspirants to the ministry. He lived in Honolulu on a notably comfortable scale. Dr. Hyde was bitterly hostile toward Catholic missionaries.

Dr. Hyde's Letter

Dr. Hyde took to his pen after Damien's death, when the news arrived that, under the patronage of the Prince of Wales, a committee had been organized in London to perpetuate the name of the leper priest.

Thereupon, Dr. Hyde wrote to his colleague, Rev. H. B. Gage, the following open letter:

Honolulu, August 2, 1889

Rev. H. B. Gage,

Dear Brother, in answer to your inquiries about Father Damien, I can only reply that we who knew the man are surprised at the extravagant newspaper laudations, as if he was a most saintly philanthropist. The simple truth is, he was a coarse, dirty man, headstrong and bigoted. He was not sent to Molokai, but went there without orders; did not stay at the leper settlement (before he became one himself), but circulated freely over the whole island (less than half the island is devoted to the lepers), and he came often to Honolulu. He had no hand in the reforms and improvements inaugurated, which were the work of our Board of Health, as occasion required and means were provided. He was not a pure man in his relations with women, and the leprosy of which he died should be attributed to his vices and carelessness. Others have done much for the lepers, our own ministers, the government physicians, and so forth, but never with the Catholic idea of meriting eternal life.

Yours, etc.,
C. M. Hyde

The letter was reproduced in many quarters of the globe with considerable effect.

To parry this attack, the Picpus Fathers prepared long, irrefutable arguments and sent some to the press.

The Bishop of Honolulu himself took up his pen. He declared that after an investigation of the facts, he was warranted in guaranteeing the integrity of his late missionary. He made it a point also to remind the world that in the course of sixteen years Damien had not been in Honolulu for a total of two months in all.

The leper Hutchinson, who had lived on Molokai since 1876, made himself the spokesman for all his companions at the leprosarium and told the world that the Reverend Mr. Hyde "was from the first to last nothing but an out and out liar."

In a brief critical study in three parts, Father Albert came to the defense of the priest with whom he formerly had been associated on Molokai and established both the innocence of Father Damien and the baseness of his accuser. The doctor, he said in the terms of St. Paul, was a worldly man "incapable of understanding any of the things that are of the spirit of God." Father Albert also emphasized the fact that no ministers had ever set foot in the lazaretto, with the exception of one, who had had his eye on publicity through the press. Besides, the single visit of this gentleman had been of short duration. "He leaned over some of the sick, keeping a safe distance from actual contact; he had the prudence to avoid entering any of the huts; and with the derisive laughter of the lepers in his ears, he regained his boat with inappropriate speed." There had indeed been one non-Catholic pastor at the lazaretto, but he was a Kanaka leper who had no choice but to reside in the leper settlement. His works of zeal had not shaken the world.

Then, of a sudden, the Picpus Fathers ceased firing, for it was no longer necessary for them to defend their confrere. Robert Louis Stevenson had waded into the thick of the fight with his letter in reply to Dr. Hyde. After the trumpet blast of the distinguished Scottish author had gone echoing around the world, there was nothing left of Dr. Hyde's charges and precious little of the doctor himself.

At the time, Stevenson was living in Tahiti. During a sojourn in Honolulu, he had taken the opportunity to visit Molokai, where he spent eight days inspecting the leprosarium with the practiced eye of a professional writer. Upon reading Dr. Hyde's letter in an Australian newspaper of October 26, 1889, he replied with his famous open letter.

The author of *Treasure Island* and so many other well-known books intended that this letter, bearing absolutely independent and unsolicited testimony, be included in his *Complete Works*. Stevenson addressed himself to Dr. Hyde, but appeals to the heart of the world.

Stevenson's Testimony

Sydney, February 25, 1890

Sir,

It may probably occur to you that we have met, and visited and conversed; on my side, with interest. You may remember that you have done several courtesies, for which I was prepared to be grateful. But there are duties which come before gratitude, and offenses which justly divide friends, far more acquaintances. Your letter to the Reverend H. B. Gage is a document which, in my sight, if you had filled me with bread when I was starving, if you had sat up to nurse my father when he lay a-dying, would yet absolve me from the bonds of gratitude....

For it is in the interest of all mankind and of the cause of public decency in every quarter of the world, not only that Damien should be righted, but that you and your letter should be displayed at length, in their true colors, to the public eye.

> To do this properly, I must begin by quoting you at large: I shall then proceed to criticize your utterance from several points of view, divine and human, in the course of which I shall attempt to draw again and with more specification the character of the dead saint whom it has pleased you to vilify; so much being done, I shall say farewell to you forever.

After having copied out the letter of Pastor Hyde, Stevenson continues.

> To deal fitly with a letter so extraordinary, I must draw at the outset on my private knowledge of the signatory and his sect.... And this is perhaps the moment when I may best explain to you the character of what you are to read: I conceive you as a man quite beyond and below the reticencies of civility; with what measure you mete, with that shall it be measured you again; with you, at last, I rejoice to feel the button off the foil and to plunge home. And if in aught that I shall say I should offend others, your colleagues, whom I respect and remember with affection, I can but offer them my regret; I am not free, I am inspired by the consideration of interests far more large; and such pain as can be inflicted by anything from me must be indeed trifling when compared with the pain with which they read your letter. It is not the hangman, but the criminal, that brings dishonor on the house.
>
> You belong, sir, to a sect—I believe my sect, and that in which my ancestors labored—which has enjoyed, and partly failed to utilize, an exceptional advantage in the islands of Hawaii.... This is not the place to enter into the degree or causes of their failure, such as it is. One element alone is pertinent and must be plainly dealt with. In the course of their evangelical calling, they—or too many of them—grew rich. It may be news to you that the

houses of missionaries are a cause of mocking on the streets of Honolulu. It will at least be news to you, that when I returned your civil visit, the driver of my cab commented on the size, the taste and the comfort of your home. It would have been news certainly to myself, had anyone told me that afternoon that I should live to drag such matter into print. But you see, sir, how you degrade better men to your own level; and it is needful that those who are to judge betwixt you and me, betwixt Damien and the devil's advocate, should understand your letter to have been penned in a house which could raise, and that very justly, the envy and the comments of the passers-by. I think (to employ a phrase of yours which I admire) it "should be attributed" to you that you have never visited the scene of Damien's life and death. If you had, and had recalled it, and had looked about your pleasant rooms, even your pen perhaps would have been stayed....

I am persuaded your letter was inspired by a certain envy, not essentially ignoble and the one human trait to be espied in that performance. You were thinking of the lost chance, the past day; of that which should have been conceived and was not; of the service due and not rendered *Time was*, said the voice in your ear, in your pleasant room, as you sat raging and writing; and if the words written were base beyond parallel, the rage, I am happy to repeat—it is the only compliment I shall pay you—the rage was almost virtuous. But, sir, when we have failed and another has succeeded; when we have stood by and another has stepped in; when we sit and grow bulky in our charming mansions and a plain uncouth peasant steps into the battle under the eyes of God and succors the afflicted in his turn and dies upon the field of honor—the battle cannot be retrieved as your unhappy irritation has suggested. It is a lost battle, and

> lost forever. One thing remained to you in your defeat—some rags of common honor; and these you have made haste to cast away.
>
> Your Church and Damien's were in Hawaii upon rivalry to do well; to help, to edify, to set divine examples. You having (in one huge instance) failed and Damien succeeded, I marvel it should not have occurred to you that you were doomed to silence; that when you had been outstripped in that high rivalry and sat inglorious in the midst of your well-being, in your pleasant room—and Damien, crowned with glories and horrors, toiled and rotted in that pigsty of his under the cliffs of Kalawao—you, the elect who would not, were the last man on earth to collect and propagate gossip on the volunteer who would and did.

Stevenson then explained to Dr. Hyde his use of the word "pigsty" as a hyperbolic expression. However, he admitted it was not a complete exaggeration to use the expression "a coarse and dirty man." R. L. S. was not loath to depart from "the conventional halo and the conventional features so drawn by men who have not the eye to remark or the pen to express the individual.... For the truth that is suppressed by friends is the readiest weapon of the enemy." He would substitute a portrait that was accurate but none the less admirable. The letter continues:

> You may ask on what authority I speak. It was my inclement destiny to become acquainted, not with Damien, but with Dr. Hyde. When I visited the lazaretto, Damien was already resting in his grave. But such information as I have, I gathered on the spot in conversation with those who knew him well and long: some indeed who revered his memory; but others who had sparred and wrangled with him, who beheld him with no halo, who

> perhaps regarded him with small respect and through those unprepared and scarcely partial communications the plain human features of the man shone on me convincingly. These gave me what knowledge I possess; and I learnt it in that scene where it could be most completely and sensitively understood—Kalawao, which you have never visited, about which you have never so much as endeavored to inform yourself; for, brief as your letter is, you have found the means to stumble into that confession. "*Less than one-half* of the island," you say, "is devoted to the lepers."

At this point in his letter, Stevenson described the physical appearances of the peninsula upon which the leprosarium was set.

> With this hint you will now be able to pick out the leper station on a map; you will be able to judge how much of Molokai is thus cut off between the surf and the precipice, whether less than a half, or less than a quarter, of a fifth, or a tenth—or say, a twentieth; and the next time you burst into print you will be in a position to share with us the issue of your calculations.
>
> I imagine you to be of those persons who talk with cheerfulness of that place which oxen and wainropes could not drag you to behold. You who do not even know its situation on the map, probably denounce sensational descriptions, stretching your limbs the while in your pleasant parlor on Beretania Street. When I was pulled ashore there one early morning, there sat with me in the boat two sisters, bidding farewell (in humble imitation of Father Damien) to the lights and joys of human life. One of these wept silently; I could not withhold myself from joining her. Had you been there, it is my belief that nature would have triumphed even in you; and as the boat drew but a little nearer, and you beheld the stairs crowded with

abominable deformations of our common manhood and saw yourself landing in the midst of such a population as only now and then surrounds us in the horror of a nightmare—what a haggard eye you would have rolled over your reluctant shoulder towards the house on Beretania Street!...

I do not think I am a man more than usually timid; but I never recall the days and nights I spent upon that island promontory (eight days and seven nights), without heartfelt thankfulness that I am somewhere else. I find in my diary that I speak of my stay as a "grinding experience"; I have once jotted in the margin, "*Harrowing* is the word"; and when the *Mokolii* bore me at last towards the outer world, I kept repeating to myself, with a new conception of their pregnancy, those simple words of the song—"*Tis the most distressful country ever yet was seen!*" And observe: that which I saw and suffered from was a settlement purged, bettered, beautified: the new village built, the hospital and the Bishop House excellently arranged; the sisters, the doctor and the missionaries, all indefatigable in their tasks. It was a different place when Damien came there and made his great renunciation and slept that first night under a tree amidst his rotting brethren: alone with pestilence; and looking forward (with what courage, with what pitiful sinkings of dread, God only knows) to a lifetime of dressing sores and stumps....

Damien shut too, with his own hand, the doors of his own sepulcher.

Here Stevenson quoted some extracts from a diary he had kept while he was in Molokai. They list Damien's faults, which the writer had investigated, collecting his data "from the lips of those who had opposed the father in his life."

A. Damien is dead and already somewhat ungratefully remembered in the field of his labors and sufferings. "He was a good man, but very officious," says one. Another tells me he had fallen (as other priests so easily do) into something of the ways and the habits of thought of a Kanaka; but he had the wit to recognize the fact and the good sense to laugh at it. A plain man it seems he was; I cannot find he was popular.

B. After Ragsdale's death (Ragsdale was a famous Luna, or overseer, of the unruly settlement), there followed a brief term of office by Father Damien, which served only to publish the weakness of the noble man. He was rough in his ways and he had no control. Authority was relaxed; Damien's life was threatened and he was soon eager to resign.

C. Of Damien I begin to have an idea. He seems to have been a man of the peasant class, certainly of the peasant type: shrewd, ignorant and bigoted, yet with an open mind and capable of receiving and digesting a reproof if it were bluntly administered; superbly generous in the least thing as well as in the greatest, and as ready to give his last shirt (although not without human grumbling) as he had been to sacrifice his life; essentially indiscreet and officious, which made him a troublesome colleague; domineering in all his ways, which made him incurably unpopular with the Kanakas, but yet destitute of real authority, so that his boys laughed at him and he must carry out his wishes by means of bribes. He learned to have a mania for doctoring; and set up the Kanakas against the remedies of his regular rivals: perhaps (if anything matters at all in the treatment of such a disease) the worst thing that he did, and certainly the easiest. The best and worst of the man appear very plainly in his dealings with Mr. Chapman's money; he had originally

> laid it out (intended to lay it out) entirely for the benefit of Catholics, and even so not wisely; but after a long, plain talk, he admitted his error fully and revised the list.

Is this a faithful portrait of Damien? It was drawn by a neutral observer who was unhampered in his investigation. If the picture seems to be unflattering, it should be remembered that Stevenson drew his information from those who were not of Damien's faith.

The import of the word "bigot" as applied to Damien should be clarified. It signifies that the priest was zealous in his apostolate, that he tried to communicate his faith, motivated by the conviction of its absolute truth. In the eyes of non-Catholics who look upon all Christian churches as equally true, a Catholic priest bent upon converting others is clearly a "bigot."

In connection with the criticism of his "practice" of medicine in competition with regular physicians, it should be noted that there were several periods in the "medical" career of Father Damien: the first period, when the lepers had no doctors at all; the second period when, in the words of the superintendent, "doctors were never there when needed"; and the third period at the beginning of which, in 1886, Dr. Mouritz came to reside at the lazaretto. Certainly, no fault can be found with Father Damien for having cared for the abandoned sick. In the second period, the visiting physicians on returning to Molokai after an interval spent in Honolulu quite conceivably might have found fault with the medical care exercised in their absence: a doctor is inclined to think that his patient might have been saved if only he himself had been present. The criticism we are discussing has some merit only when applied to the third period; for Damien could have been less reluctant to yield his beloved and long-established "clientele" to the new resident physician, Dr. Mouritz. In the course of time, under the pressure of more or less subtle hints, the priest withdrew from his "practice," and his relations with the medical man became more and more correct.

That non-Catholic physician, Dr. Mouritz, gave four years of professional service to the leprosarium. Here is his word-picture of Damien: "He was of a nervous-choleric temperament and had abundant black hair. He had a powerful baritone voice, sang very well, was more handsome in profile than full-face and usually went bareheaded. He was stiff and sensitive. During his long years at Molokai, he had come to act like an autocrat; and, if left to him, the leprosarium might have become a sort of monastic institution under his conscientious dictatorship."

We return to Stevenson's letter. In its final section, it takes up and refutes, point by point, the accusation of Dr. Hyde.

> Damien was *"coarse."*
>
> It is very possible. You make us sorry for the lepers who had only a coarse old peasant for their friend and father. But you, who were so refined, why were you not there, to cheer them with the lights of culture? Or may I remind you that we have some reason to doubt if John the Baptist were genteel; and in the case of Peter, on whose career you doubtless dwell approvingly in the pulpit, no doubt at all he was a "coarse, headstrong" fisherman! Yet even in our Protestant Bibles Peter is called a saint.
>
> Damien was *"dirty."*
>
> He was. Think of the poor lepers annoyed with this dirty comrade! But the clean Dr. Hyde was at his food in a fine house.
>
> Damien was *"headstrong."*
>
> I believe you were right; and I thank God for his strong head and heart.
>
> Damien was *"bigoted."*
>
> I am not fond of bigots myself, because they are not fond of me. But what is meant by bigotry, that we should

regard it as a blemish in a priest? Damien believed his own religion with the simplicity of a peasant or a child; as I would I could suppose that you do. For this, I wonder at him some way off; and had that been his only character, should have avoided him in life. But the point of interest in Damien, which has caused him to be so much talked about and made him at last the subject of your pen and mine, was that, in him, his bigotry, his intense and narrow faith, wrought potently for good and strengthened him to be one of the world's exemplars.

Damien *"was not sent to Molokai; but went there without orders."*

Is this not a misreading? Or do you really mean the words for blame? I have heard Christ, in the pulpits of our Church, held up for imitation on the ground that his sacrifice was voluntary. Does Dr. Hyde think otherwise?

Damien *"did not stay at the settlement, etc."*

It is true he was allowed many indulgences. Am I to understand that you blame the father for profiting by these, or the officers for granting them? In either case, it is a mighty Spartan standard to issue from the house on Beretania Street; and I am convinced you will find yourself with few supporters.

Damien *"had no hand in the reforms, etc."*

...I have now come far enough to meet you on a common ground of fact; and I tell you that, to my mind not prejudiced by jealousy, all the reforms of the lazaretto, and even those which he most vigorously opposed, are properly the work of Damien. They are the evidence of his success, they are what his heroism provoked from the reluctant and the careless. Many were before him in the field; Mr. Meyer, for instance, of whose faithful work we hear too little: there have been many since; and some had more worldly wisdom, though none had more devotion, than our saint. Before his day, even you will confess, they had effected little. It was his part, by one striking act of martyrdom, to direct all men's eyes on that distressful country. At a blow, and with the price of his life, he made the place illustrious and public. And that, if you will consider largely, was the one reform needful, pregnant of all that should succeed. It brought money; it brought (best individual addition of them all) the sisters; it brought supervision, for public opinion and public interest landed with the man at Kalawao. If ever any man brought reforms, and died to bring them, it was he.

Damien *"was not a pure man in his relations with women, etc."*

How do you know that? Is this the nature of the conversation in that house on Beretania Street which the cabman envied, driving past?—racy details of the misconduct of the poor peasant priest, toiling under the cliffs of Molokai?

Many have visited the station before me; they seem not to have heard the rumor. When I was there, I heard many shocking tales, for my informants were men speaking with the plainness of the laity; and I heard plenty of complaints of Damien. Why was this never mentioned? And how came it to you in the retirement of your clerical parlor?

But I must not even seem to deceive you. This scandal, when I read it in your letter, was not new to me. I had heard it before; and I must tell you how. There came to Samoa a man from Honolulu; he, in a public-house on the beach, volunteered the statement that Damien had "contracted the disease from having connection with female lepers"; and I find joy in telling you how the report was welcomed in a public house. A man sprang to his feet; I am not at liberty to give his name, but from what I heard I doubt if you would care to have him to dinner in Beretania Street. "You miserable little ____!" (here is a word I dare not print, it would so shock your ears). "You miserable little ____!" he cried. "If the story were a thousand times true, can't you see you are a million times lower, for daring to repeat it?"

I wish it could be told of you that when the report reached you in your house, perhaps after family worship, you had found in your soul enough holy anger to receive it with the same expressions: aye, even with that one which I dare not print; it would not need to have been blotted away, like Uncle Toby's oath, by the tears of the recording angel; it would have been counted to you for your brightest righteousness. But you have deliberately chosen the part of the man from Honolulu, and you have played it with improvements of your own. The man from Honolulu, miserable, leering creature, communicated the tale to a rude knot of beachcombing drinkers in a public-house, where (I will so far agree with your temperance opinions) man is not always his noblest; and the man from Honolulu had himself been drinking—drinking, we may charitably fancy, to excess. It was to your "Dear Brother, the Reverend H. B. Gage," that you chose to communicate the sickening story; and the blue ribbon which adorns your portly bosom forbids me to allow you the extenuating plea that you were drunk when it was done....

But I fear you scarce appreciate how you appear to your fellow men; and to bring it home to you, I will suppose your story to be true. I will suppose—and God forgive me for supposing it—that Damien faltered and stumbled in his narrow path of duty; I will suppose that, in the horror of his isolation, perhaps in the fever of incipient disease, he, who was doing so much more than he had sworn, failed in the letter of his priestly oath—he, who was so much a better man than either you or I, who did what we have never even dreamed of doing—he too tasted of our common frailty. "O Iago, the pity of it!" The least tender should be moved to tears; the most incredulous to prayer. And all that you could do was to pen your letter to the Reverend H. B. Gage!

Is it growing at all clear to you what a picture you have drawn of your own heart? I will try yet once again to make it clearer. You had a father: suppose this tale were about him and some informant brought it to you, proof in hand: I am not making too high an estimate of your emotional nature when I suppose you would regret the circumstance? That you would feel the tale of frailty the more keenly, since it shamed the author of your days? And that the last thing you would do would be to publish it in the religious press? Well, the man who tried to do what Damien did, is my father, and the father of the man in the Apia bar and the father of all who love goodness; and he was your father, too, if God had given you grace to see it.

After that devastating letter, Dr. Hyde and his friends dropped out of sight. Four years afterward, however, upon hearing of Stevenson's death, some of them deemed it opportune to break silence with the announcement that in the closing days of his life Stevenson had repented of having written his classic letter. In their presumption, however, they had overlooked the existence of the writer's widow. Mrs. Stevenson used the public press to categorically deny the new fabrication. Indeed, she said, far from retracting his letter, Robert Louis Stevenson had only this regret on his deathbed, that he had not borne down harder on the defamers of the leper priest. Thereupon, these rash ranters again withdrew into silence.

The saintly priest had been made aware that tales were being circulated that reflected on his chastity. Some intimations had been given him a short time before his death. He accepted this heartache, as he had accepted all his other pains, without signs of bitterness or indignation, without retaliation. There was this advantage, however, in his being informed: he took advantage of such occasions as presented themselves to defend his reputation.

For example, a specialist in leprosy, Dr. Morrow from New York, had asked him to describe the progress of his disease. About one month before he went to the judgment-seat of God, namely, on March 10, 1889, Damien dictated to Dutton a statement calculated to satisfy the curiosity of the learned visiting physician. Into this report crept these two sentences: "In my family, there has never been a case of syphilis. I myself have never had intimate relations with any person whatsoever." He had made this declaration spontaneously, and he insisted that Dutton record it exactly as he had spoken it. When Dutton had made the final copy, Damien read the statement carefully. Then, at the bottom of the last page, as testimony of the truth of the text, he wrote in his own handwriting:

> *Strictly correct!*
> J. Damien de Veuster
> Catholic priest.

Moreover, he would have been pleased to have an autopsy performed on his body after his death. Poor priest, would it have been in the hope that the evidence of such an examination would oblige even willful doubters to accept the fact of his innocence?

Chapter 17

Servant of the Lord

It is the considered judgment of directors of souls that another's conscience cannot be sifted and that the last judgment alone will reveal the full harvest of sainthood.

Hence, it would be rash to think of drawing the mystic portrait of a man who had no time for contemplating his own virtues and left no diary of the operations of grace in his soul. The reader, therefore, must personally evaluate Damien's sanctity according to what the leper priest said and what he did. We shall not go beyond noting some of his psychological and spiritual traits.

A "Special Kind" of Holiness

The Protestant author, Robert Louis Stevenson, prophesied that within a century Rome would declare this leper a saint. As early as August, 1889, a few months after Damien's death, his bishop wrote to the father general: "I regard him as a real saint, though of a special kind." Perhaps his lordship was hinting that this man was a saint who had put him to considerable bother? Nearer the mark, he probably meant that the priest had practiced his religion in the best way possible, that is, by employing to the limit of his powers the peculiar combination of disposition and of grace bestowed on him by God.

As a family heritage and as a concomitant of his great purity of soul, Damien enjoyed the gift of unassailable faith. He had no more doubt concerning the reality of the supernatural order than he had concerning the visible world around him. He regarded unbelievers and heretics with the same concern and charitable commiseration as a man bursting with health regards a friend laid low by illness. Not the least uncertainty of mind troubled him. Contemplation of the four last things, of the final judgment of God and of eternal sanctions was habitual with him. His letters and his talks echo his daily meditations on the end of human life. It was his staunch faith that determined his vocation, sustained him in his labors and sufferings, consoled him in his sorrows and directed all his deeds.

The learned Dr. Hyde, who had met Damien in 1885, tagged him as "ignorant." It is true that it would have been futile to expect him to turn aside from his relief work among the lepers to grapple with thorny problems. In fact, he had in him no spark of curiosity about questions in the speculative order. The Gospels, the teachings of the Church, the synopsis of theology in his notebooks furnished him with all the answers he needed.

Damien was genuinely devout. He loved God with all his heart; he served him with zeal and perseverance; and he blessed him for the gift of his high vocation, accepting with the same filial trust both the joys and the concerns that sprang from it.

Having dedicated himself to the Sacred Hearts of Jesus and Mary, the objects of the special veneration of his congregation, he nourished a manly devotion for Christ, who by his life and passion has saved us, and to the Virgin Mother of Christ, who dispenses the treasures of divine mercy.

He gave himself diligently to prayer, wherein he received

the light and consolation with which heaven favors the pure of heart and the humble of mind. Pure he was to the point of scruple. Humble he remained despite the world-wide adulation which his works of zeal evoked.

All who knew him attest to his long periods of prayer at the beginning and at the close of each day. He said his Mass and recited his office up to the very day his failing eyesight robbed him of those priestly consolations. His free moments found the rosary in his hands. He even resorted to stealing time from the hours of the night to converse with God.

"The cemetery, the church and the priest-house are set in close proximity on the same plot of ground," he wrote. "I am the sole warder, during the night, of the beautiful garden of the dead wherein my children lie at rest. It is my delight to go there to say my rosary. Take my word for it, the cemetery and the huts of my dying sons are my finest books of meditation, nourishing my own heart and furnishing food for my sermons."

Father Damien had nothing in common with those pious people whose practice falls short of their profession. He was a thoroughly honest man, to whom any thought of lying or deceiving or fawning was always abhorrent. Indeed, his rectitude sometimes bordered on the naive. He could not impute to others the base or selfish motives he rejected for himself.

Father Jourdan's biography of Damien shows the priest of Molokai exactly fulfilling all the duties of his state of life, going beyond the letter of the rule rather than falling short, relaxing none of the ties that bound him to his congregation, obeying his superiors whatever their command and whatever the cost to him.

There was, for example, the order that came to him to cease welcoming some Mormons who, probably, were imposing on him. Without hesitation, he informed the persons concerned:

Kalawao, February 1, 1880

Gentlemen,

Please be good enough to tell your leader at Laie that my bishop has directed me to stop following my customary practice and to receive no more of your people who may come to visit the leprosarium in the future. This order is not at all to my taste, but I beg your indulgence for my desire to put obedience to my superior above all other considerations.

He gave his provincial an exact accounting of his personal expenditures, precise to the smallest details: "$.25 for an ax-handle, $.50 for a broom, $.50 for a wood-basket, $.50 for a knife, $1.50 for a spade, $2.00 for tobacco."

Damien drew up a daily schedule for his observance. Undoubtedly it was often bent, under the stress of frequent emergency, but in the main it served, as intended, to regulate all his actions as though he were living in a monastery:

Five o'clock—visit to the church as soon as possible after rising; morning prayers; adoration; meditation: to half-past-six.

Six-thirty—Mass; instruction; thanksgiving; to half-past seven. Then, attention to sundry matters touching the welfare of the faithful.

Eight o'clock—breakfast followed by a little conversation and arrangement of domestic affairs.

Nine o'clock—recitation of Little Hours on the verandah.

Half-past nine—spiritual reading, followed by study or correspondence.

Twelve o'clock—visiting the sick in such ways as to make the circuit, once every week, of all the huts in the settlement. If I manage to return by five o'clock, then recitation of Vespers followed by disposal of any domestic business that has piled up.

Six o'clock—supper. As evening falls, Rosary, breviary and evening prayers.

Between nine and ten-o'clock—Bed.

It seems hardly necessary to dwell on his matchless charity. His close friends affirmed that he "was always expressing his gratitude for the slightest services." More to the point, he had that genuine gratitude that remembers benefactors of former days from whom nothing further may be expected. He never forgot any of those who had helped him in the early years of his studies and of his religious life. He was faithful to his friends and to his kin.

His filial devotion to his father showed itself in manly encouragements to follow the Christian road mapped out for the head of a family. For his mother, exhortation was superfluous. He strove to console and sustain her, perhaps bringing a smile to her lips as he tried to persuade her that, among his lepers, he was the happiest and most serene man in the world. In a letter to his mother in 1880, he said: "I imagine that you must be getting to look like your mother, who was my godmother at Haecht, as she was thirty years ago. Perhaps, you, too, now need a cane to get to church. She was a little touchy on that score. Don't be like her. Do as I do and always keep one handy!" But it suddenly occurred to him that he had said too much. His mother might begin to picture him as so fatigued or diseased as to need to hobble around on a stick. It would never do to put that idea into her head! "From the picture I am sending to you, you will see that I am still the big Joe that I used to be. My constitution is still good. Besides, when fatigue threatens me, I harness my horse to the four-wheeled carriage I got as a gift from the government."

In contrast to the many idealists who start life generous in spirit but are driven by the perversity of human beings to cynicism and hardness of heart, Damien became ever more kind, more tolerant and more merciful as his work for his fellow men progressed. In his first days on the island, he had written of the Protestant pastors as if they were his adversaries. Later on, however, he spoke of them without a trace of irritation: "I try to be on friendly terms with everybody. I know of only one leper who bears a grudge against me. He is a former minister, who takes pleasure in writing supposedly anonymous articles against me.... I forgive him from my heart. May the good Lord also pardon him!"

Some people forgive but do not forget. Damien kept no register of insults received; and even those who were most persistent in denouncing him had no occasion ever to fear retaliation from him. On the other hand, when it was he who had occasioned the upset mind or the wounded heart, he lost no time in seeking pardon. He was hasty; he was impulsive. Herein, so far as we can judge, lay his predominant fault, against which he waged a lifetime of stubborn warfare. When investigators came around asking whether his temperament ever got the upper hand, the lepers replied, "Sometimes, certainly, but he became exasperated only when our misconduct called for it. And even at those times, he apologized – although it was clearly not his duty to do so."

Those who wish to draw up a complete record of Damien's faults will not fail to note that he lacked order and organizing ability. As the saying goes, he allowed himself to be eaten out of house and home. Even the children twisted him around their fingers. He found it difficult to be harsh with those little lepers doomed to an early death.

A letter to Pamphile gives a picture of an orphanage run, as some today would say, democratically:

"After Mass, I receive a packet of letters, among which I spy yours. What self-denial it is to devote a half hour to thanksgiving as usual before opening your letter! During this half hour, I pray at length for all our family, but with distractions coming from all sides. Thanksgiving over, I become so absorbed in my mail that I forget all about lighting my oil stove to make the coffee. Your excellent idea of writing only good news gives me great pleasure. All around me, witnessing my signs of joy, stand my orphans; and since they are inquisitive, they don't give me time to take a breath. I must translate every line for them as I read it, give them all the details, tell them of your provincial's visit to you, of your 5,782 pages of sermons and of our good old mother and her grandchildren.... To make a long story short, we got through the morning; but that day there was no breakfast, so I combined it with dinner; and then, stick in hand, I set forth to visit my sick."

Among the many qualities the attentive reader cannot have failed to observe, Damien had two that were especially helpful to him as a man of action.

One was his genuine singleness of purpose—his having but one objective in mind and moving steadily toward it without distraction. As a realistic peasant who gave each man his due but allowed no one to impose on him and ascribed no importance to passing fancies, Damien wasted little time on talk or needless formality; he got to the heart of a matter as though by instinct; he thrust aside obstacles and started to do the job in the most effective and most expeditious way. Before advisers and even the official warders of the purse strings had had time to discuss or postpone it, the job had been finished.

And finally, his optimism! In this world one runs into good and evil, beauty and ugliness, and forms one's attitude toward them. The pessimist concerns himself chiefly with the defects and disasters of the world. Snapping his fingers at that dark view of things, the optimist chooses to concentrate on the pleasant aspects of this old world and cheerfully gets on with his work. Such an optimist was Damien, and such an optimist he remained. Nothing ever reduced in him that inner strength which is the fruit of optimism and the virtue of hope. He went his way pursuing his mystical vision, yet executing his charitable designs, repairing what he saw could be salvaged, losing little time over sterile regrets and retaining almost to his final hours the same vitality and the same passion for action as in the glowing hours of his apostolic youth.

Chapter 18

Death and Renown

Before his death, Damien had the happiness of seeing sisters established at the lazaretto.

For fifteen years he had pleaded to have them. “If only I had a dozen nursing sisters here!” he wrote in 1873. “How much good they would do!”

However, at that time it was considered inhuman to expose women to the risk of contracting leprosy. For a long time even the most charitable souls had shrunk from the prospect of living among lepers as from something more repugnant than human nature could stand. It was, in large measure, the example of Damien that made women aware of a type of heroism to which they could truly aspire.

Nevertheless, the king, the queen, Prime Minister Gibson, the Board of Health and the physicians were as one in their desire that sisters come to assist in the care of the lepers. In 1883, Dr. Fitch, a physician in attendance at Molokai and at Kakaako, wrote this to the bishop: “I am a Protestant...but in the matter of seeing that food is properly prepared, that children are well cared for, and especially that the love of virtue and the practice of chastity are high in popular esteem, I do not know of anyone to equal the sisters." He went further and put himself to much trouble to raise the funds required to bring nursing sisters to Hawaii.

Appeals were dispatched to forty-seven congregations. Twenty-two made no reply; twenty-three replied that they felt the project was impossible; only two sent an answer that permitted further negotiation.

The Franciscan Sisters of Syracuse, NY., were the first to actually accept the assignment. On November 9, 1883, seven sisters from this community arrived in Honolulu. Four of the seven were stationed at the hospital at Kakaako; and three at the hospital at Wailuku on the Island of Maui. Not one of them was sent to Molokai!

Sisters for Molokai

Up to the year 1888 Damien's pleas that some of these sisters be assigned to the lazaretto fell on deaf ears. But out of the blue came a development that finally led the bishop to satisfy Damien's request. With the approval of the government, Mr. B. C. Bishop, a Protestant banker in Honolulu, announced his plan to found an orphan asylum for girl lepers at Kalaupapa. He desired that the projected institution be under the direction of sisters; and he requested, as a step toward securing them, that recourse be had to the bishop at once.

At about this very time the rumor arose that some Anglican sisters in England were aspiring to this post of self-sacrifice and were ready to begin the long journey. Faced with this complication, the bishop asked the sister superior at Kakaako to send some of her sisters to Molokai at once.

Three were chosen: Mother Marianne, Sister Leopoldine and Sister Vincentia. On November 14, 1888, they landed at the lazaretto to undertake the direction of the Bishop Home. Damien emerged from his sick-room, to which fever had confined him for six weeks, and hurried down to the pier in his carriage to welcome them. A few days later, a Picpus priest, Father Wendelin Moller, came to join them. He had been appointed pastor at Kalaupapa.

Mother Marianne was a rare combination of keen intellect and warm heart. She and her sister companions made it their chief concern to surround with thoughtful attention and affectionate veneration the battle-scarred veteran who was even then on the brink of his grave.

In this late evening of Damien's life, God was inclining his face toward him and consoling him with manifest blessings. He was giving him the greatest comfort possible for a man of action who finally arrives at the point of exhaustion: the comfort of seeing at long last that his battle has not been in vain and that other hands will grasp the sword that he must lower. Abbé Conrardy was to be his successor at Kalawao. One of his confreres in the Congregation already occupied the post at Kalaupapa. And finally, like so many angels sent from heaven, here were the daughters of St. Francis, come to adopt his leper children.

Mother Marianne has left us an account of one scene:

> He also took us to the girls' orphanage at Kalawao. "My children," he said, "I shall soon be dead, but you will not be left alone. The sisters whom you see before you have come to take care of you. They are going to take you with them to Kalaupapa." All the girls burst into tears of desolation; but they finally allowed themselves to be led away. Two of them, however, could not be torn away; they clung to his feet like leaches and cried, "Father, we want to stay with you until we die." He had to yield to their tearful entreaty. Not until after his death was it possible to fetch these two. They then followed us without resistance to the Bishop Home, where they, too, died a short time later.

> He also took us to the boys' orphanage and showed us the method of sewing trousers for the boys....
>
> While we were visiting Father Damien in the last hours of his life, he turned suddenly and asked us, "Will you take care of my boys when I am no longer with them?" Three times he repeated this question. We gave our promise...and we have kept our word.

What Mr. Bishop had done for girls, another Protestant gentleman of Honolulu, Mr. Baldwin, did a little later for boys. The Baldwin Home became the counterpart of the Bishop Home, and through these two institutions the whole juvenile population benefited from the motherly devotion of the sisters.

Damien could die in peace. "My day is over," he told the sisters. "I can die now; you will carry on the work far better than I could hope to have done it."

The methods of the sisters were indeed an improvement over his: their attentiveness in matters of hygiene and cleanliness was more meticulous; their precautions against the danger of infection were more efficacious. It was all quite novel to him, but he was careful to avoid interfering. He forced himself to remember that he was a leper, and when his memory slipped, he lost no time in making up for his fault.

Now Sister Leopoldine takes up the thread of reminiscence:

> We did not yet have a chapel at the Bishop Home, but we had turned a large room there into an oratory in which the Blessed Sacrament was reserved. One day when some task or other took me into the garden, I walked out of the building by the rear door and found Father Damien in the yard. He was kneeling there on a heap of refuse, with his eyes fixed on the oratory window, adoring the Blessed Sacrament. In my surprise, I gave a

little cry. Perhaps he interpreted it as a sign of repugnance. He rose immediately and humbly asked pardon for having put himself, a leper, in my way. His charity stirred me even more than his piety.

On another occasion, he had invited us to come to see the new church at Kalawao that he was hurrying to finish before death overtook him. I went there with Sister Vincentia. Our Mother had forbidden us to accept anything from him. When Father offered us some refreshments, we told him of the orders that had been given us. But he pressed the food on us, saying that his non-leper cook had prepared all of it. He feared all the time, I believe, that the good woman would take offense at our refusal. We satisfied our conscience on that score and took the food he had offered us.... The very next day, Father came to Kalaupapa and knelt before Mother Marianne to ask her pardon for having urged us to disregard her instructions.

Easter with the Lord

That was perhaps the last time that Damien set foot outside Kalawao.

He himself had been watching the advance of his disease and knew that his final hour was not far off. He wrote to Clifford: "I have been steadily yielding the last flickers of vitality, and have drawn much nearer to the cemetery." A short time later he informed Dr. Woods: "My face and hands are already decomposing."

He began to dispose of the few articles that had been reserved for his use. He transferred the aged William, the horse owned by the Mission, to his assistant priest: "Today," he wrote to his provincial on February 16, 1889, "I have sold to Father Conrardy my bay horse together with the saddle, bridle, etc., for $25.00." He bequeathed to his bishop—with the understanding that they should be dispensed according to the intention of the donors—the balance of dollars and pounds sterling which still remained in the bank. When Damien had concluded this, he said, "How happy I am, now that I have given everything away and have no burden left!"

"I should have liked to see my bishop once more," he wrote to a friend, "but the good Lord is calling me to keep Easter with himself." For some time, now, the bishop had been mellowing. He had responded to the New Year greetings from his leper priest by sending him a meerschaum pipe and an affectionate letter: "In return, I wish you," wrote the bishop, "for many years to come all the spiritual and corporal happiness compatible with the will of God, together with abundant rewards in eternity. The devil will still try mightily to hinder the work of the good by sowing dissension, but let us hope that the Lord will assist us in our weakness and lead us all to good in the end."

The provincial, however, was made of harder material; and he did not make his dying subject's load any lighter. "Don't be so positive in your notions," he wrote to Damien on January 28. On March 18, he wrote: "You have once more dipped your pen in bitterness"—this with reference to a letter from Damien in which there was not even a trace of bitterness.

With the coming in of March, the condition of the sick priest suddenly worsened.

According to Hutchinson, Damien's leprosy was of "the tubercular or cutaneous type (which) attacked his fingers, ears and chin." And Dutton adds, "He became the most repulsive leper in the lazaretto."

On March 9, the nodes burst open and running abscesses began to form. The leper took to his bed, a pallet placed on the floor of his room on the second floor. He who had received so many alms and dispensed so many gifts to his fellow men, now lay in absolute destitution. He owned not even a change of linen or sheets for his bed. Fever wracked his body, which was rolled in a cheap blanket. It was with difficulty that his friends prevailed upon him to move into a bed they had brought into his room.

Brother James Sinnet attended Father Damien to his dying breath. Father Conrardy and Brother Joseph Dutton were frequently at his bedside, and kindly Mother Marianne often slipped over from Kalaupapa to visit him. As for the other lepers, Brother James just found it impossible to keep them out of the sick-room. From England, Chapman and Clifford sent most affectionate messages. Father Damien asked a companion to write them that they remained in his innermost thoughts and in his prayers.

In the presence of Brother Dutton on March 10, he denounced vehemently the calumnies that had been spread abroad concerning him, and he called on heaven to witness his innocence.

From Mother Judith, his old friend in Honolulu, he received a letter on March 19 (St. Joseph's Day), conveying good wishes for his name day and congratulating him on the twenty-fifth anniversary of his coming to the Hawaiian Islands.

Damien himself wrote to Dr. Smith, the resident physician at the lazaretto:

> Dear Sir,
>
> If it is convenient for you, please call to see me. I am anticipating some discomfort in the lower intestines. Do this favor for your very feeble
>
> J. Damien.

He persisted in reading his office as long as he had any eyesight left. From this time, the condition of his hands prevented his saying Mass. "Every night," recalled Sinnet, "as soon as the hour of eleven had sounded, he asked me to begin the prayers before Communion. He joined in with devout fervor. At a quarter to twelve, I went to awaken Father Conrardy, who slept on the ground floor, and we went to the church to get the Blessed Sacrament. On our return, I walked ahead with my lantern in my hand. Father Damien communicated with the ardor of a seraph."

Sleep now fled from him, except for an hour or two in the night. He slept with his mouth wide open, for the corruption had invaded his wind-pipe and was spreading rapidly. His voice had dropped to a hoarse whisper.

The ax had been laid to the root of this mighty oak. This man of forty-nine, checked in his full vigor, was now but a ruin. In the midst of his valiant struggles, the stout-hearted wrestler had been thrown. Leprosy had strangled him and floored him when victory was in sight. The disease had long degraded and mocked the exterior of his body; now it was ravaging within, eating away his lungs, stomach and intestines.

On March 25, his provincial brought coals to Newcastle: "Be calm, now, Father," wrote the superior, "and do as the others do!"

This counsel of patience was completely uncalled for. Eyewitnesses assure us that the sufferer's resignation did not falter. His eyes, which were being closed inexorably by a ghastly swelling, he kept fixed upon Burne-Jones' painting of St. Francis with his stigmata, which hung on the wall above his bed. All the troubles of his conscience had disappeared. His heart was grateful and his mind serene.

"I move gently toward my grave," he had a companion write to Chapman and Pamphile. "It is God's will, and I am very grateful to him that I am dying of the same disease and in the same way as my flock. I am very happy; I have my heart's desire."

His sufferings and his preparation for his great journey did not keep him from thoughts of his young people. The last lines Damien scrawled summoned the doctor to the bedside of one of them:

> Dear Sir,
>
> Jobo Puhomamia has been spitting blood. Try to snatch a moment to go to see him. He lives in the second house beyond that of James Lewis. Do this courtesy for your friend,
>
> J. Damien.
>
> In the same house you will also find the dying woman of whom I spoke to you last evening.

Father Wendelin and Abbé Conrardy administered the last sacraments to him. Father Wendelin related:

> On March 30, I heard his general confession, then I made my own confession to him. Together, we renewed the vows of our religious profession. "Don't you represent our congregation so far as I am concerned?" he asked me. "Then, when you write to the father general, don't fail to tell him how happy I am to die a son of the Congregation of the Sacred Hearts!"
>
> On the next day, Sunday, March 31, he received Holy Viaticum. In the course of the day he manifested joy at the approach of death. "You see my hands," he said. "All the wounds are healing and the crust is becoming black. You know that's a sign of death. Look at my eyes, too. I've seen so many lepers die that I can't be mistaken.... The Lord is calling me to keep Easter with himself."

He received the anointing of the sick on April 2, from the hands of Father Conrardy. "How good God is," he said in the course of the day, "to have preserved me until I could have two priests at my side in my last moments and also the good Franciscan Sisters at the lazaretto. Now I can sing my *Nunc dimittis*. The work for the lepers is in good hands and I am no longer necessary, so I shall go up yonder."

"When you're up there," someone said, "you won't forget those you're leaving behind as orphans?"

"Oh, no! If I have any credit with God, I'll intercede for everyone in the leprosarium."

His confrere, Father Wendelin, begged Damien, like Elijah, to leave to him his mantle, so that he might share in his courage. Damien did not consider himself Elijah.

"Why, what would you do with it?" he asked. "You couldn't wear it. It's full of leprosy!"

"I asked for his blessing," continued Father Wendelin, "which he gave me with tears in his eyes. He also blessed the brave daughters of St. Francis for being the answer to his fervent prayers to have sisters at the lazaretto."

For some days following, a little improvement might be noted. Lepers who came to say farewell found their priest wrapped in blankets and seated in a chair. He who had been all driving activity, now rested motionless and serene. He thanked them affectionately for their visit and arranged a rendezvous with them in heaven. They were deeply impressed by the joy shining in his eyes.

"On Saturday, April 13," wrote Father Wendelin, "his condition became very bad and he lost consciousness from time to time. He received Communion for the last time a little after midnight. He recognized me when I approached his bed. As the Sunday services at Kalaupapa required my presence there, we bade each other farewell, and I left him. I returned the next day, but he was delirious. On the morning of Monday, April 15, I got a note from Father Conrardy telling me that Father Damien was in his agony. I set out for Kalawao at once, but on the road I was met by a messenger, coming to announce his death." Gently, with a smile, the leper priest had breathed his last in the arms of Brother James, "like a child who falls asleep." He had gone to God at the beginning of Holy Week, a few days before Easter, as he had foretold.

A Name That Echoes On

His body was once again clothed in his cassock. Soon the blemishes of leprosy disappeared from his face and the sores on his hands dried up. Toward eleven o'clock the corpse was taken to the church, where it lay in state until the following day, surrounded by lepers, who prayed through their tears. In the afternoon, the Franciscan Sisters lined his plain coffin with white silk and covered the outside with black cloth.

Next day the funeral was solemnized. Save for the overwhelming grief of the congregation, it differed little from those over which Damien himself had presided at Kalawao several times a week. When Mass was over, a procession headed by a cross moved slowly into the cemetery and passed under a large flag hanging from the pandanus tree that had been so dear to the dead priest. First in line came the musicians of the band and the members of the confraternities; then the sisters with the women and the girls from the Bishop Home; then the coffin borne by eight lepers, followed by the two priests with their acolytes, Brothers James and Joseph with their orphans and the rest of the male population.

Father Damien had expressed the desire to sleep his last sleep under the tree which had sheltered him during his first nights on Molokai. His wish was respected. At the foot of that tall pandanus he was buried; and there for forty-seven years he rested among those whom he had loved.

Above his grave, the Mission set a cross of black marble bearing the inscription:

V.C.J.S.
Sacred to the Memory
of the Revd. Father
Damien de Veuster
Died a Martyr to his Charity
For the afflicted Lepers
April 15, 1889
R.I.P.

Two weeks after the death of Father Damien, at services conducted in the cathedral of Honolulu, Bishop Kockeman rose to the occasion by delivering a funeral oration that was in all respects a panegyric.

Throughout the world, without distinction of party or of editorial policy, the praises of the press soared above even those spoken by the dead priest's bishop. Never before, perhaps, had the people of this earth witnessed so unanimous a demonstration of sincere homage to a Catholic priest. In every village and town that boasted a newspaper, the death of the Father of the Lepers was announced; thousands of articles fervently commemorated his heroism and his martyrdom; and in a few short months Father Damien's name was on the lips of men in every quarter of the globe.

Since that day hundreds of books and brochures have told his life; statues have been raised in his honor; poets and musicians have paid him tribute; his name has been given to streets, to magazines, to colleges training for the missions and to establishments serving the leper.

Although it has had ramifications over all the earth, his popularity has struck its deepest roots in English-speaking countries. Encyclopedias cannot ignore him; and works dedicated to the great benefactors of humanity speak of him in the same breath as Abraham Lincoln and Louis Pasteur.

In a world of abounding merit, why has Father Damien

remained an object of universal homage?

Has the glory of the Apostle of Molokai flourished because the writings of Robert Louis Stevenson, who rose to his defense, are still widely read?

Is it the dramatic aspect of his adventure that has struck the imagination and touched the heart? The world had heard the harrowing cry of the lepers abandoned on a rock set in the ocean; and it had admired him who, in answer to that Macedonian plea, had gone to bury his young manhood in that pit of putrefaction. It had seen Damien, himself now a leper, driven from his bed of pain to wander through the night, rosary in hand, among the graves of the fellow-lepers he had buried. It had been stirred to the core to learn that, after many hardships and labors, a man gentle and humble of heart had gone to his death disfigured by leprosy and befouled by calumny, yet blessing God for his lot.

Whatever its source, the renown of Damien has suffered no loss with the passage of time. This priest has his firm niche as an imitator of Christ in his love for all mankind. Before Damien, people pretended to forget that lepers were human. His example made men blush for their cruelty and bend again to their duty. From his day, lepers have ceased to be treated as outcasts; they are no longer driven from the helping hands extended to all other sufferers; and the human race no longer bears the shame of casting from its bosom the most wretched of its children.

On June 19, 1889, the future Edward VII, then Prince of Wales, summoned to his palace the Committee for the Leprosy Fund, of which he had expressed the desire to be patron. In the course of his address, he said:

> The life of Father Damien and his heroic death not only have given birth to the most ardent sympathy throughout the United Kingdom, but they have stirred us still more profoundly to follow in a measure his ex-

> ample.... The people who require our assistance are not unknown to us, nor are they foreigners.... They are, like us, subjects of the English Crown, inhabitants of India and of our colonies, all of whom in strict justice have on us a claim that the Hawaiians did not in their turn have on the faithfulness of the young priest who gave his life for them!
>
> To discharge our debt to him, I put before this Committee a proposal for a memorial embracing three projects:
>
> The first is the erection of a monument dedicated to his memory at Molokai on the very spot where he made his sacrifice and where his remains repose.
>
> The second is the founding of an establishment named after him and designed for the exclusive study of the horrible disease of leprosy and for the preparation of the facilities required by those who will undertake the voyages that such a study will entail.
>
> The third is the launching of a comprehensive and searching inquiry into the condition of lepers in India and in all other parts of the far-flung British Empire.

This program was carried through to the letter. The monument to Father Damien took the form of a large cross of red granite which was unveiled on September 11, 1893. On its lower part had been set a medallion of white marble with a head of Father Damien in high relief above the inscription: "The greatest proof of love man can give is to give his life for his friends."

However loyal they may be to the memory of the dead, survivors do not always find it desirable to respect the wishes of the departed in full. Father Damien's repose among his lepers on Molokai was only temporary.

In 1936, the Belgians announced their intention of claiming the remains of their fellow-countryman; and at the request of King Leopold III, President Roosevelt lent a willing hand to the project. On January 27, the corpse of the leper priest was exhumed. The body was found to be emaciated but intact, save for some finger-joints that had been destroyed in the course of his illness. His hair was still in place—black with silver threads.

The coffin was transported to Honolulu on a bomber escorted by nine other planes. In the Hawaiian capital, full official honors were paid to the remains. Then the casket was brought down to the harbor and placed aboard the American ship *Republic* for the first leg of its journey. At Panama, the Belgian ship *Mercator* received the precious burden and carried it to Antwerp, where it arrived on May 3.

The humble missionary made a triumphal return to this native land. The Belgian king, the members of the government, the hierarchy and an enormous crowd of people turned out to receive him. When the *Mercator* and her escort of small craft with fluttering flags drew alongside the quay, trumpets sounded in salute, the troops presented arms and all the bells of the city burst into clamor. A tall hearse drawn by six white horses bore the casket to the cathedral, where solemn funeral services were conducted in the presence of the civil and religious dignitaries of the land.

Late that same evening, an automobile, moving at low speed, carried the casket to Louvain. Under the stars of that night Damien for the last time followed a once familiar route; he traversed the countryside where he had worked as a youth; he passed once again before the shuttered houses of his native village, before the school where he had learned to read, before the church where he had knelt in his boyhood, before the gates of the cemetery in which his father and mother were sleeping. Toward midnight he arrived at the very place from which he had set out, seventy-three years before, to march to his destiny. He found his journey's end in the chapel of the Picpus Fathers just under the cell in which Pamphile had died. Beneath a beautiful monument of black marble, he rests there awaiting the resurrection.

Epilogue

A Miraculous Cure

A few years after Father Damien's death, the acclaim given to the hero of Molokai was seconded by a sign of divine approval.

In February, 1895, Simplicia Hue, a Picpus Sister stationed at San Servan, became ill with influenza, which developed into a series of violent gastro-intestinal attacks accompanied by internal hemorrhaging. Her condition became grave, and at one point during the ensuing months she thought to be near death. Unable to consume anything except a little milk, the thirty-seven-year old sister grew extremely weak. When able to walk, she could do so only with a cane, because of the pain.

On September 8, Sister Simplicia confidently began a novena to Father Damien. Placing before her a small picture of Damien as a leper, she prayed three Our Father's, Hail Mary's and Glory's, adding the invocation: "Father Damien, pray for us and cure me." She kept the picture with her and kissed it often out of devotion. During the first three days of the novena, however, Sister's condition worsened so that she could not receive Holy Communion. Her nights were sleepless because of the pain.

On September 11, which was the worst day of all, Sister Simplicia prayed to Father Damien with even greater confidence. That evening, worn out by pain and fatigue, she fell asleep.

At 1:30 a.m. on September 12, Sister Simplicia awoke to discover that she was lying on her painful side and with no discomfort at all. She felt that she had been cured and excitedly called the nurse. Then she got up and walked around the room with no pain. She returned to bed and rose about three hours later to walk again.

The community was making its annual retreat, which Sister Simplicia had eagerly looked forward to. Feeling well, she went to chapel to attend the retreat conference. Then she took a walk in the garden and afterwards joined her companions in the dining room, where she was able to eat normally.

The doctor confirmed that no natural explanation could be given for an almost instantaneous healing of an ulceration of the colon that had continued for six months without improvement.

After her cure, Sister Simplicia resumed her customary, varied duties: picking fruit, working in the laundry and serving in the dining room. She lived thirty-two more years – as far as is known, without any recurrence of the same illness. She died of tuberculosis at age seventy-one.

When this information was submitted in support of Father Damien's cause for beatification, the following points were noted:

1. The prognosis was unfavorable; witnesses agreed that the case was serious.

2. No appropriate therapy had been found; any treatments used had resulted in only slight improvement at best.

3. Father Damien de Veuster had been explicitly invoked.

The cure was instantaneous or almost instantaneous, and all signs of the illness disappeared.

After recovering her health, Sister Simplicia lived for thirty-two more years without a relapse of the same illness.

St. Paul Book & Media Centers

ALASKA
750 West 5th Ave., Anchorage, AK 99501; 907-272-8183
CALIFORNIA
3908 Sepulveda Blvd., Culver City, CA 90230; 310-397-8676
5945 Balboa Ave., San Diego, CA 92111; 619-565-9181
46 Geary Street, San Francisco, CA 94108; 415-781-5180
FLORIDA
145 S.W. 107th Ave., Miami, FL 33174; 305-559-6715
HAWAII
1143 Bishop Street, Honolulu, HI 96813; 808-521-2731
ILLINOIS
172 North Michigan Ave., Chicago, IL 60601; 312-346-4228
LOUISIANA
4403 Veterans Memorial Blvd., Metairie, LA 70006; 504-887-7631
MASSACHUSETTS
50 St. Paul's Ave., Jamaica Plain, Boston, MA 02130; 617-522-8911
Rte. 1, 885 Providence Hwy., Dedham, MA 02026; 617-326-5385
MISSOURI
9804 Watson Rd., St. Louis, MO 63126; 314-965-3512
NEW JERSEY
561 U.S. Route 1, Wick Plaza, Edison, NJ 08817; 908-572-1200
NEW YORK
150 East 52nd Street, New York, NY 10022; 212-754-1110
78 Fort Place, Staten Island, NY 10301; 718-447-5071
OHIO
2105 Ontario Street (at Prospect Ave.), Cleveland, OH 44115; 216-621-9427
PENNSYLVANIA
214 W. DeKalb Pike, King of Prussia, PA 19406; 215-337-1882
SOUTH CAROLINA
243 King Street, Charleston, SC 29401; 803-577-0175
TEXAS
114 Main Plaza, San Antonio, TX 78205; 210-224-8101
VIRGINIA
1025 King Street, Alexandria, VA 22314; 703-549-3806
GUAM
285 Farenholt Avenue, Suite 308, Tamuning, Guam 96911; 671-649-4377
CANADA
3022 Dufferin Street, Toronto, Ontario, Canada M6B 3T5; 416-781-9131; 1-800-668-2078